GET AHEAD IN...

PHYSICS

from

NEWTON'S LAWS

to **LEVITATING**

FROGS

ILLUSTRATED BY

TOM WHIPPLE **JAMES DAVIES**

CONTENTS

GET AHEAD IN...
PHYSICS

**FOR MY DAD, WHO STARTED PATIENTLY ANSWERING
MY SCIENCE QUESTIONS AS SOON AS I COULD TALK –
AND HASN'T STOPPED SINCE – T.W**

FOR MOS – J.D

First published 2020 by Walker Books Ltd
87 Vauxhall Walk, London SE11 5HJ

2 4 6 8 10 9 7 5 3 1

Text © 2020 Tom Whipple
Illustrations © 2020 James Davies

The right of Tom Whipple and James Davies to be identified as
author and illustrator of this work has been asserted by them in
accordance with the Copyright, Designs and Patents Act 1988

This book has been typeset in Sabon, Intro Black and Amasis

Printed and bound in UK

British Library Cataloguing in Publication Data: a catalogue record
for this book is available from the British Library

ISBN 978-1-4063-8824-4

www.walker.co.uk

WALKER
BOOKS

FSC
www.fsc.org
MIX
Paper from
responsible sources
FSC® C020471

INTRODUCTION

Do I really need another Physics textbook?

You don't. The one you have is fine. I'm sure it covers everything you need for your exams. And yet...

And yet what?

Well, I'm sure it tells you, say, in the electricity chapter, that:

V = IR

Current is the flow of electrons

Mains AC transmits a sinusoidal waveform at 50hz

That's all correct, and all stuff you need to know.

Great, so I'll just reread it.

You could, of course. But let's be honest – it's hard.

Physics is a wonderful subject. It's about how the universe works, from the smallest atom to the largest black hole. This is a majestic, soaring, inspiring branch of knowledge that is also (whisper it) ... occasionally a bit boring.

And this book isn't?

I hope not. For instance, that stuff about electric current? We only know about that because of an experiment from hundreds of years ago. And I think the science is easier to remember, once you've heard the story.

Why's that?

Because they electrified a bunch of monks.

Monks? As in, the sort who pray?

Exactly. In eighteenth-century France, the abbot of a monastery made his poor old monks hold hands. Then he electrified them.

In this book, I'm going to tell you why –
and, at the same time, explain a bit of the
Physics you need to know for your exams.

So this book is useful because it includes
stories about clerical torture?

Yes!

Um, not just that. There are
also levitating frogs.

And don't forget the farting cows. (Cows are
very useful for the particle theory of matter.)

No, no, I wouldn't forget them...
Where are you going with this?

The point is, this book is not meant to
be a *replacement* for a revision guide.
It's meant to be an *assistant* to one.

It tells you how we got to where we are, and
why – and hopefully, along the way, will help
you to remember the most important details.

Details like?

Well, specific latent heat is technically: "the amount of energy in the form of heat required to completely effect a phase change of a unit of mass."

It's also the reason why, during the Second World War, a British lord accidentally shot a US admiral in the leg.

Will there still be equations, as well as grumpy admirals?

Not many. Certainly, not as many as you'll find in your textbook.

Each chapter is tied, though, to a key topic for learning Physics. By the end, you will have covered the whole syllabus – building on and deepening the knowledge you already have.

Great! So I can forget the equations.

No, definitely not. Textbooks – and teachers! – are very useful. They have a lot of information that they need to pass on.

Sometimes, in doing so, it isn't always possible to share the stories of the people behind that information: the women and men who saw further, thought deeper, worked harder or (to give another example) stuck needles in their eyes to see how light works.

That's where this book comes in.

So onto Chapter One – which means it's time for some farting cows...

CHAPTER 1

PARTICLE THEORY OF MATTER

INTRODUCTION
PARTICLE THEORY OF MATTER

IN THIS CHAPTER YOU WILL LEARN ABOUT:

- How everything is made of particles
- Density
- Temperature
- Solids, liquids and gases
- Conservation of mass
- Gas pressure
- Brownian motion

BEFORE YOU READ THIS CHAPTER:

What is the world made of?

Imagine you took a lump of metal, or ice, or anything really, and cut it in half.

Then imagine you cut that half in half again. And again. And again.

When would you stop? Could you keep on going forever – or would you eventually reach something so small that it can no longer be cut?

Nowadays, we know the answer to all this: that everything around us is made from particles.

Some of these particles are called atoms. Atoms are the smallest building blocks of any pure material. For example, an atom of iron is the smallest bit of iron you can have, while still calling it "iron". (And a pure material, like iron, is called an **element**.)

Some of these particles are called **molecules**. Molecules are two or more atoms, bonded together.

For instance, water is made from hydrogen and oxygen; so, a molecule of water is two hydrogen atoms and one oxygen atom joined together. If you break them apart, it stops being water.

But early scientists didn't know this. They soon realised, though, that if particles did exist, then a lot of things – from melting ice to chemical reactions – made a lot more sense.

This chapter is about what we now call the **particle theory of matter.**

To understand why it was such a revolutionary idea, let's start in the most logical place: cow farts.

CONSERVATION OF MASS

Over the course of four days, a calf farts out 14 g of a gas called methane. We know this because, one day, some scientists decided to collect all the methane exiting a calf's bottom and weigh it.

Not just that, they weighed its poos (272 g), its urine (10.1 kg), and – after crawling around on the bottom of its enclosure to collect every remaining trace – its dandruff (28 g).

At the end, they had two numbers. The first was the total weight that went into the enclosure, including milk, water, oxygen and the calf itself: 52.5 kg. The second was the total weight at the end: 52.5 kg.

Nothing had changed. Between the gas out the front, the gas out the back, the digestion and the milk slurped up, everything weighed the same.

REARRANGING OF PARTICLES

Think about how amazing that is. A collection of chemicals goes into a calf. Inside the calf, some liquid changes to gas, some to solid(ish) cow poo, and some gas gets combined with other chemicals to make the calf a bit bigger.

At the end of this whole process, everything is exactly the same mass.

More than that, early chemists who studied similar reactions noticed something even more puzzling. When the calf farts, it does so with exquisite control.

Methane is made from carbon and hydrogen atoms – and each rattling trumpet from its bottom produces methane with a perfect and unwavering ratio of one part carbon to four parts hydrogen. Why is this always the case?

Why do you never get methane with ever so slightly more hydrogen in it or ever so slightly less carbon?

CARBON

HYDROGEN

There is a way to explain both phenomena – the conservation of cow mass and the perfect ratio of a cow fart. That explanation is particles.

Imagine if everything going into a cow is particles and everything coming out of a cow is the same particles, just rearranged.

2 Some particles entering the cow split up and join with other particles – making milk and muscle.

3 Others are rearranged to be farther apart, changing to gas.

4 Carbon from grass and hydrogen from water become CH_4 in methane.

WATER

1 H_2O in water, carbon, nitrogen and other elements in grass.

Whatever happens though, the number and kind of atoms in is the same as the number and kind of atoms out. The reason the mass does not change is because the particles don't change. They are always there, just in different positions.

UNWAVERING RATIOS

The particle theory also makes it obvious why the ratio of elements in chemicals such as methane is always precisely the same too.

Methane is what happens when one carbon particle gets together with four hydrogen particles. These form their own methane particle – a molecule – that bounces around as a gas. So methane is a collection of particles that, by definition, has one carbon and four hydrogens – maintaining an absolutely perfect and constant ratio.

When the particle theory was first proposed, no one could prove it was correct (spoiler: it is), but they could see it explained so much. For instance, it tells us what heat is.

METHANE

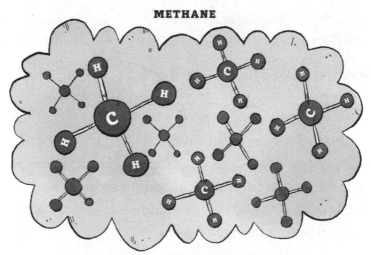

Each carbon is attached to four hydrogens.

HOT THINGS HAVE BOUNCIER PARTICLES

If everything is made from particles, then heating things just makes their particles jiggle about – heating is the process of giving a particle something called **kinetic energy** (see Chapter Two). When you touch a hot cooker and go "ow", the pain is from the particles in it bashing into your hand.

It also tells us why substances change state.

If particles are tightly bonded together in a solid object, then heating them will eventually make them jiggle so much the bonds break and that object becomes a liquid.

Heat them a bit more, and the particles jiggle so much they break free of each other entirely and form a gas.

BALLOONS ARE INFLATED BY PARTICLES HITTING THE SIDES

It tells us what gas pressure is too.

Why is a balloon taut? Why do your ears pop when you go in an aeroplane? It's because the pressure of the gas is different.

A balloon contains gas with a higher pressure than the atmosphere, and the gas pressure of the atmosphere is higher on a runway than up in the air.

But what is pressure?

If gas is just a bunch of jiggling particles – which it is – then gas pressure is a result of those particles hitting the side of their container, whether that be the rubber of a balloon or your ear drum.

The hotter they get, or the more there are, the more often particles bash against the sides – and we feel that as "pressure".

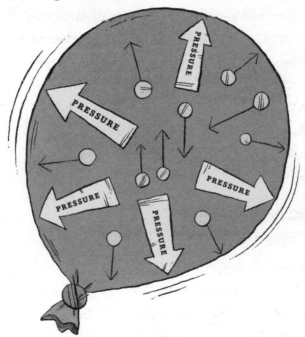

It also tells us that if those gas particles come from a cow's bottom, then it is best to retreat to a safe distance – before they jiggle their way into your nose.

WHAT IF ICE SANK?

Imagine the scenario. There you are enjoying a nice cold drink on a nice warm day, when suddenly something very odd happens in your glass. Your ice plunges, without warning, to the bottom.

The same happens at the same time around the world. In the Antarctic, some seals get an unexpected bath when the ice floe they are lounging on disappears. In the North Atlantic, the wreck of the *Titanic* suffers the final indignity of having an iceberg sink on top of it. But the odd thing is not, when you think about it, that all this ice is sinking – it's that it ever floated in the first place.

Because water does not behave as any sensible material should.

A substance is at its most spread out when it is a gas. All its particles are far apart, so its **density** is low.

Density is a way of saying how many particles there are in a given volume. The more there are (and the heavier they are), the denser something is.

If you cool a substance down, the particles move a bit less and are able to join together a bit more, becoming a liquid. Its particles are closer together, so it is more dense.

As you cool the liquid, its particles slow down and – as they whizz about less – they are able to fit in a smaller space. They keep fitting into smaller and smaller spaces, until the material becomes a solid.

THE EXCEPTION TO THE RULE

Unless, that is, the substance is water. Water particles behave sensibly all the time they are a gas, and almost all the time they are a liquid.

But if you cool them below four degrees Celsius, something very strange happens: instead of the water getting more dense, it becomes less.

Because of the odd crystal-structure it forms as it solidifies, the water particles are pushed farther apart.

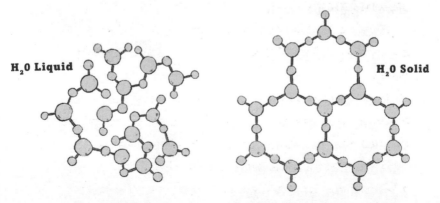

As water becomes ice, it spreads into a crystal lattice.

This means that a kilogram of liquid water takes up less space than a kilogram of solid water – better known as ice.

This also results in something miraculous to which we probably owe our lives: ice floats. If ice sank, then the world would be very different – different enough that it is extremely unlikely humans would have evolved.

In oceans, lakes and rivers, ice would form not at the top but at the bottom. It would then grow upwards until it reached the top – forming a solid block and leading to some very sad fish flapping about on the surface.

So every winter, the aquatic life in cold regions would be destroyed.

And, perhaps slightly less relevantly, on a hot summer's day you would have a drink that is cold at the bottom, rather than the top.

BROWNIAN MOTION

An atom is very small. It is roughly a hundred millionth of a centimetre across, depending on the element. That means you would need to have a clump of material about 100,000 atoms thick before you would even be able to see it.

Yet, 2,000 years ago the Roman Lucretius saw atoms. And you can see them too – or, rather, you can see what they do.

In a poem, Lucretius told readers to look into a sunbeam and watch tiny dust particles "tumbling in the light". There, caught in the sun, the particles' movement is jittery and apparently random.

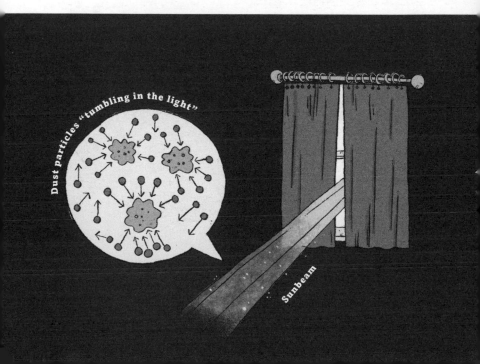

He thought the movement was not random at all. It was a sign that they were being battered by what he called "the primal stuff" – also known as molecules and atoms.

Molecules and atoms which, we now know, are always on the move.

"Secret and viewless", he said, these atoms "lurk beneath" – their unseen blows causing a chain of motion that bashes bigger and bigger particles until we humans can at last see the result, in the bouncing of dust.

His theory was absolutely right. Unfortunately, the world was not ready to hear it.

AHEAD OF HIS TIME

The centuries would pass. The Roman Empire would fall, Christianity and Islam would rise. China would go on to invent gunpowder and printing. In Africa, Timbuktu would become a great centre of learning on the edge of the Sahara.

JEAN BAPTISTE PERRIN

A hundred generations of humans would live their lives, seeing dust particles dancing in light – and thinking nothing of it.

It was only in the nineteenth and early twentieth centuries that scientists – among them Albert Einstein – would once again look into a sunbeam and wonder what was making the dust jump.

They worked out that there was only one explanation: the dust was being hit by atoms.

In 1926, one of them, a Frenchman called Jean Baptiste Perrin, won a Nobel Prize for this incredible deduction.

Really, he should have shared it with Lucretius.

IN SHORT: Everything we see, smell or taste is just an arrangement of particles. Even cow farts.

WHAT YOU NEED TO KNOW:

- All matter is made of **particles**, which are always moving.
- The more particles there are in a specific volume the **denser** the material gets. **Density** is **mass** per unit volume (see Chapter Five for mass).
- A material that has a billion particles per cubic metre at 20° Celsius might have half as many in the same volume at 100° Celsius because the particles move faster and farther apart at a higher temperature … which makes it less dense.
- In **solids**, the particles are packed close together and can't move much. In **liquids** the particles are close together but randomly arranged, moving around and past each other. In **gases** the particles are far apart and move quickly in all directions.
- **Temperature** measures how much particles are moving on average.
- The **pressure** of a gas is the collective force with which they hit the side of a container.

So that's the particle theory of matter! Did you find it all a bit easy? Good – then you're ready for the next bit. At the end of each chapter is a section that takes it a bit further: a glimpse of the Physics that lies beyond.

WHAT YOU DON'T NEED TO KNOW, BUT MIGHT LIKE TO:

PLASMA

So I think I get it now. Everything is made of particles.

When they are far apart they are gas. When they are closer together they are liquid. When they are so close they can join together they are solid.

Exactly.

And those are all the states of matter.

Nope.

Sigh. Go on.

There's also plasma.

What's plasma?

An ionized gaseous substance in which the nuclei are adrift in a malleable sea of electrons.

Oh … um, good? Is it pretty rare?

Not exactly. It might well be the most common form of ordinary matter in the universe.

How come I haven't seen it then?

Actually, you have. Plasma is the substance that glows in neon lights, that is created by lightning – and also that fills stars.

But what is it? If the other states of matter depend on how hot a substance is, where does plasma fit in? Is it cooler than a solid? Hotter than a gas?

Normally the latter, but that's not the best way of thinking about it. Plasma is what happens when the particles themselves change.

Right. The entire idea of the particle theory of matter is there are these indivisible units, that remain unchanged and unchanging.

Yes.

And now you say they change?

Yes. Sorry about that. Atom particles are made of smaller particles – electrons, protons and neutrons (see Chapter Three).

Some of the electrons can be stripped from the particles and move around freely. This leads to plasma, a substance with very strange properties.

It can glow, conduct electricity, and – in a plasma screen TV – show you what's going on in the football. You can even make it in your microwave.

Ooh, how?

With a blown-out match, a cup and … actually, don't make it in your microwave.

Or, if you do, don't blame me when you cease to have a microwave.

OK. I definitely won't search for YouTube clips of how to make a ball of mysterious glowing matter in my microwave.

Because doing that would be grossly irresponsible and not in any way a lot of fun.

Good.

Anyway, now it all really does makes sense. So to recap, there are four states of matter – solid, liquid, gas and plasma.

And Bose-Einstein condensate.

Bose what?

The fifth state of matter. When supercooled bosons...

You know what?

What?

Can I make it in a microwave?

No.

Let's leave it.

CHAPTER 2

ENERGY

INTRODUCTION
ENERGY

IN THIS CHAPTER YOU WILL LEARN ABOUT:

- The types of energy
- Conservation of energy
- Efficiency
- Specific heat capacity
- Conductors and insulators
- Work and power

BEFORE YOU READ THIS CHAPTER:

Where something – anything! – interesting is happening, it is because energy is changing.

Energy is the thing that heats stuff up or makes it move. Life, television, sunshine, rock music, motor racing, spiders eating flies … it's all about energy.

And so is Physics itself.

This chapter is about how energy is transferred from one temporary home to another.

That's everything from heat to movement and even to "potential energy" – a concept that sounds pretty silly, until you have experienced a bit of it. For instance, you might experience it in the form of an apple – after the potential energy from it being high in a tree is converted to movement energy, and it falls down to hit you on the head.

The chapter is also about how energy is stored and conserved. Because that apple's energy will still be around, in some form, at the end of the universe…

A PERPETUAL MOTION MACHINE

In the summer of 2017, a British scientist died and left his family a really annoying inheritance. For months it just sat there on their mantelpiece, a bicycle wheel in a box that kept turning and turning, and they didn't know what to do with it.

It was a perpetual motion machine. And the reason it was annoying is because every scientist knows perpetual motion machines are impossible.

Yet here one was – a machine that never needed charging but never stopped. With each cycle of the wheel, it taunted the world's physicists.

The British scientist, Dr David Jones, had built it decades earlier, and invited people to guess its secret: none did. He knew as well as anyone that none of this was possible.

And he thought it was an excellent practical joke.

DR DAVID JONES

THE PERPETUAL MOTION MACHINE

WHY THE MACHINE COULDN'T EXIST, EVEN THOUGH IT DID

The most important thing in the universe, which his bicycle wheel was making a mockery of, is **energy**.

Viewed in one way, life itself is just about the transfer of energy – from the Sun into plants, from plants into animals, from animals into other animals ... i.e., into *you*. Survival is about two things:

1. Making sure you take in as much energy as you use (taking in less is known, to use less technical language, as "starvation").
2. Making sure that something else – a lion, say – doesn't view you as a little parcel of walking energy, and decide to consume that energy (in a transfer known, more colloquially, as "lunch").

The crucial rule about energy, which is measured in a unit called a **joule,** is it cannot be created or destroyed – just converted.

A wind turbine converts kinetic energy, which is the energy of motion, from moving air into electrical energy. That electrical energy then goes along wires in your kitchen into your cooker, and is converted into heat energy.

But along the way, some energy is transferred to other, less useful, stores. As the turbine's blades turn, they make a swishing sound and heat up a little bit – all that heat and sound is wasted energy. As the cooker heats up, it also rattles a bit – that too is lost energy.

And this is what brings us to the bicycle wheel. As the wheel turns, it must be pushing aside air molecules. So the energy of its own motion is being transferred into the motion of air.

At its hub, there must be a little bit of friction – that friction will cause the metal to heat up, meaning some of the turning energy is also being converted to heat energy.

In any machine, at any stage, the amount of its energy being converted into useful energy – such as a spinning wheel – is its **efficiency**. And its efficiency is never 100 per cent.

A WHEEL CAN'T TURN FOR EVER

So no matter how carefully it is built, the wheel is losing energy. If it is losing energy, it must be getting slower. If it isn't getting slower, then either the laws of Physics are wrong or Dr Jones hid an energy source somewhere.

He was the first to admit, right from its very creation, that this was what he had done, but he also had no intention of telling people what it was.

Some thought it harvested solar energy; some that it had a hidden battery. Maybe there was a radiation source concealed in the rim of the wheel?

In the 36 years Dr Jones's wheel spun before he died, many people tried to find out.

Its secret survived thousands of guesses and numerous competitions. It travelled the world to be inspected by the public and scientists, who were allowed to use any device or scanner to investigate it but not stop it or take it apart.

They all failed.

Before he died, Dr Jones wrote a letter that he entrusted to his friend, the scientist Sir Martyn Poliakoff. After the funeral, Sir Martyn duly opened it – excited to find the answer.

There was a problem though: Jones's printer seemed to have run out of ink. The explanation stopped halfway through.

Today, the wheel is housed in the Royal Society, the home of Britain's most distinguished scientists. None of them have yet guessed its secret.

THE CIRCLE OF LIFE – AND ENERGY

From the beginning of time until the end of time, energy is neither created nor destroyed.

The energy of the Big Bang is still distributing itself around the cosmos. The energy of a dinosaur munching on a tree is still to be found, spread thinly around the Earth and beyond.

The key thing to understand is that, along the way, this energy has been transferred – from one kind of store to many others.

65 million years ago

Outside the atmosphere, an asteroid speeds towards the Earth, unnoticed. As it falls, it gets faster and faster. It is converting **POTENTIAL ENERGY**, which is the energy it has through being high up in the Earth's gravitational field, into **KINETIC ENERGY**.

A plant is converting the Sun's light energy into **CHEMICAL ENERGY** inside itself (a process known as "photosynthesis").

Potential Energy:

Potential energy is the energy an object has because of where it is. If you put a ball on a roof, for instance, it has potential energy – because we know it can be pushed off the roof. That means it has the potential to gain kinetic energy.

The asteroid enters the atmosphere, travelling at 70,000 kilometres an hour. At this speed, air molecules don't have time to move out of the way and the friction is huge, heating up the sky. **KINETIC ENERGY** is converted to **HEAT ENERGY**.

Oblivious, a dinosaur eats the yummy plant, taking on its CHEMICAL ENERGY and storing it in its own body.

Chemical Energy:

Chemical energy is like a battery for animals. It is a way to store energy for later – for instance, as fat.

The asteroid hits the Earth and the rock vaporizes, releasing the energy of thousands of atomic bombs. There is tremendous heat and a massive boom. The asteroid's **KINETIC ENERGY** has become **SOUND** and **HEAT**.

Rather than dying instantly, a nearby dinosaur is (miraculously) sent flying in the air to land on a distant cliff. This means a bit of the asteroid's kinetic energy has become the dinosaur's kinetic energy, which has in turn become **POTENTIAL ENERGY**. The energy transferred — in this case all the kinetic energy converted to potential energy — is known by physicists as the **"WORK DONE"** on the dinosaur.

The terrible impact sends shockwaves through the atmosphere, shaking up the air molecules and causing *ELECTRICAL POTENTIAL* to build up in a nearby cloud.

Electrical Potential:
When charge builds up in a cloud, it is ELECTRICAL POTENTIAL. Similar to potential energy from gaining height, this is energy that is waiting for its moment of release – to be converted into something useful (or dangerous).

The dinosaur's luck has run out.

It is hit by lightning – the **ELECTRICAL POTENTIAL** is converted into **ELECTRICAL ENERGY**, which is in turn converted into a pretty scorched dinosaur.

The dinosaur's last act is to run towards the cliff edge. As its legs push it towards its doom, they apply what is known as a force (see Chapter Five on Newton).

The work done is, as before, the energy transferred. The faster this energy is transferred, the greater the power of those very scared dinosaur legs.

Work = energy transferred.
Work is also force x displacement
Power = work/time

At the edge, things speed up. The dinosaur now converts its **POTENTIAL ENERGY** into **KINETIC ENERGY** as it plummets to its doom.

The dinosaur sinks to the bottom of the sea, where the debris of the asteroid buries it under sea sludge and the stored **CHEMICAL ENERGY** of its fat decomposes into a black soup of crude oil.*

Millions of years later, hairless apes have learnt to walk upright, talk and create complex societies that waste their time swapping photos on social media. They discover oil and burn it in cars – converting **CHEMICAL ENERGY** to **HEAT ENERGY** and then to **KINETIC ENERGY**. They also use it to make materials like plastic – meaning that some toy dinosaurs contain real dinosaurs.

*Most crude oil comes from far less exciting dead creatures, such as plankton. But there's a chance some is dinosaur-based too.

> ### *TYPES OF ENERGY ~ A QUICK RECAP:*
>
> - **Kinetic energy**: This is energy related to movement.
> - **Heat energy:** This is related to how fast individual atoms are moving – something we experience as things being hot.
> - **Chemical energy:** Energy locked up in chemicals, that can, for example, be burned to make heat.
> - **Potential energy:** Energy waiting to be converted to another form, such as kinetic energy. For instance, a pendulum at the top of its swing, or a bungee-jumper at the top – or bottom – of her jump, has potential energy that will soon become kinetic.
> - **Electrical energy:** Energy that comes from the build-up of charge (see Chapter Four).

SPECIFIC HEAT CAPACITY

The only thing that ever scared Winston Churchill was German submarines.

In 1942, Britain was slowly exhausting its food supply. Supply ships were being torpedoed crossing the Atlantic, and the ocean was too big for the RAF to protect them – they would have run out of fuel and crashed. So once their tanks were half-empty the planes had to turn around and come back, and the convoys were on their own.

What they needed was an airport floating on the sea that could never be sunk. And a man called Geoffrey Pyke knew just how they could achieve it: with ice, and two Physics concepts – **specific heat capacity** and **specific latent heat**.

GEOFFR.
PYKE

A MELTING RUNWAY

Specific heat capacity is a far-too-complicated name for something actually really simple. It can be described in lots of ways. One way is that it is how much heat energy something can store. Or, it's how slowly something heats up or cools down – how easy it is to make its atoms start jiggling or stop jiggling.

It is measured in the energy needed to raise the temperature of a kilogram of a substance by a degree (joules per kilogram-degree).

Specific latent heat is like specific heat capacity, but it's what happens when something changes state – from solid to liquid, or liquid to gas. It's the amount of energy needed to take a kilogram of substance across that transition.

INSULATORS AND CONDUCTORS
HIGH SPECIFIC HEAT CAPACITY AND LOW SPECIFIC HEAT CAPACITY

Metals have a lot of atoms close to each other that can easily jiggle to transfer energy. They are known as **conductors**; substances that don't do that are **insulators**. Metals also have a very low specific heat capacity.

This means that if you put a metal baking tray in the oven, it will very quickly become too hot to touch. If you take it out of the oven, you will be able to pick it up a few minutes later – it doesn't store much heat and will rapidly conduct away the heat it does have.

Similarly, if you lick a metal ski pole on a cold day, your tongue will stick to it because the cold of the metal will very quickly conduct the heat of your tongue. (Don't do this.)

However, a ceramic baking tray which has a high specific heat capacity and low conductivity, will take longer to heat up – but will also take a lot longer to cool down afterwards. It stores a lot of heat, and also holds on to it.

IN HOT (OR COLD) WATER

The material with one of the highest specific capacities around is water. Its ability to store lots of heat, but also take a long time to heat up from cold, is why islands such as Britain and Japan – which are surrounded by water – are not-too-cold in the winter and not-too-hot in the summer. When it is ice it also has one of the highest specific latent heats – which is why glaciers can last a summer.

It is also why ice takes so long to melt.

In fact, ice lasts so well that some desert countries have considered towing icebergs from the Antarctic to bring fresh water for drinking. Most calculations estimate you could bring one all the way to the equator and it would still lose only half its volume.

This is what Geoffrey Pyke realized, back in 1942. Britain could build a floating island of ice, an unsinkable aircraft carrier, and in the chilly waters of the North Atlantic, which themselves take a long time to heat, it would last long enough before melting to win the war.

The navy was so desperate that they agreed, and plans began under a codename...

PROJECT HABBAKUK

In Canada, an 18-metre-long test-model was constructed using ice mixed with wood-pulp to strengthen it. When it was demonstrated for the most senior British and American officials, everyone was impressed.

The event was slightly marred when Lord Mountbatten, from Britain, fired his pistol at the model. It was so resilient that, unfortunately, the bullet ricocheted into the shoulder of the rather cross American Chief of Naval Operations.

The full-size version was never built – not because it did not work, but because it was considered too expensive. With the war being won anyway, the decision was made to cancel Project Habbakuk.

And so in Canada the model was abandoned and forgotten – left as a slowly melting demonstration of the astonishing thermal properties of water.

Very slowly melting. The war ended in 1945; it was still there two years later.

IN SHORT: Energy makes the world go round. Quite literally, actually, given that it was a big burst of energy 4.5 billion years go that set us spinning in the first place.

WHAT YOU NEED TO KNOW:

- Energy cannot be created nor destroyed – just converted.
- There are different kinds of energy: **kinetic** (movement), **heat**, **sound**, **chemical**, **light** and **potential**.
- When we try to convert energy into something we can use, some energy is lost. A wind turbine will only turn a certain amount of wind energy into electrical energy – some is lost as heat or sound.
- The proportion of energy something converts is its **efficiency**.
- **Specific heat capacity** is a measure of how much energy a substance can store – you calculate by seeing how many **joules** are required to raise the temperature of a kilogram of the material by a degree.
- **Conductors** such as metals are good at moving heat – this means that they will quickly try to equalize with their surroundings.
- **Insulators** do the opposite.
- **Work done** is energy transferred. It can also be calculated as force times distance travelled.
- **Power** is the rate of doing work – it is – "work done" divided by time taken.

SECOND LAW OF THERMODYNAMICS

Why would I want to know the second law of thermodynamics?

In case you go to a party with the scientist and novelist C.P. Snow.

But I don't want to go to a party with him.

Well … imagine you *did*.

He used to get annoyed by the way – in his view – people at the parties he went to seemed to be snooty about scientists, mocking them for not knowing much about literature.

So, in a famous lecture in 1959…

Wait, 1959? Is he still alive?

No, why?

Well I'm not likely to go to parties with him then, right? Am I safe from the second law?

As you will see, no one is safe from the second law.

Anyway, the problem is, his test is now so famous that other pesky physicists might bother you with it too.

I wouldn't want that. How do I fend them off?

In 1959, he explained how he would sometimes ask a crowd of people how many of them could describe the second law of thermodynamics.

He said, "The response was cold: it was also negative. Yet I was asking something which is the scientific equivalent of: Have you read a work of Shakespeare's?"

Is not knowing the second law of thermodynamics really the scientific equivalent of never having read Shakespeare? That makes me feel a bit stupid.

Probably not; the second law is pretty hard. It states that things become less ordered over time – another way of looking at it is that there are many more ways for things to be disordered than ordered.

Like the difference between a younger cousin's playroom at the start of the day and the end?

Pretty much. The decline of order in the playroom is called **entropy**. And the reordering of it is something that can only be done by "putting energy into the system".

Or, in this case, by you going in and tidying it.

Why is this so important? Why can't he just let us browse the canapés in peace?

It ultimately tells us that energy becomes increasingly less useful.

It starts off in an ordered form – in a spinning wheel, a litre of petrol or toys on a shelf – and then becomes dissipated and spread around…

In the case of petrol, this is as the sound of your engine, the heat of your exhaust, and the kinetic energy of your car.

This converted form of energy is inevitably less useful.

What about the other laws of thermodynamics? Why didn't C.P. Snow bother people about them?

They're a lot simpler. The first law says you can't make energy appear from nowhere. The third says you can never make something so cold that its atoms stop moving completely.

Snow had a pithy way of describing them:
1. **You can't win,**
2. **You can't break even, and**
3. **You can't get out of the game.**

What does that mean?

Essentially the laws of thermodynamics are the reason you have to eat and work and struggle. Basically, they're the reason life is hard.

CHAPTER 3

RADIATION

INTRODUCTION
RADIATION

IN THIS CHAPTER YOU WILL LEARN ABOUT:

- Atomic structure
- Elements
- Isotopes
- The types of radioactivity
- Nuclear power

There have been two great revolutions in our understanding of the nature of matter.

The first was when we realized everything was made up of indivisible particles called atoms. That was what you learned about in Chapter One: The Particle Theory of Matter.

The second revolution, the one covered in this chapter, was when we realized that those atoms weren't indivisible at all.

Atoms are themselves made of smaller particles. And, in the right circumstances, the centres of atoms can be torn apart to send those smaller particles whizzing off as something called radiation.

When they do, new atoms are formed, new kinds of "nuclear" energy break free – and strange and sometimes terrible things happen...

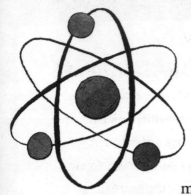

THE ATOM

Everything we see is made up of almost nothing. This book is made largely of nothing.

A big chunky bar of lead is essentially nothing. You are made mainly of nothing.

The reason we know this is because in 1909, a young physicist called Ernest Marsden was given a pointless task. Marsden was told by his boss, also called Ernest, to fire a beam of helium particles at a very thin sheet of gold, then look to see if they bounced back.

There are many things that are strange about **atomic theory.** The idea that matter reaches a stage where it becomes indivisible – so that everything can be reduced to a single atom – is far from obvious, and, as you heard in Chapter One, seemed very strange to people when it was first proposed.

But what is even stranger is that we now know, thanks to the two Ernests, that all those indivisible atoms are themselves barely there.

That was what Marsden saw that day in his laboratory. And the only reason it was him in that room was because he was the most junior member of the research team.

THE ATOM THAT WASN'T THERE

No one expected any of the particles to bounce back.

They assumed, in common with most scientists, that the atom was the same throughout. Like a potato, its matter was spread evenly through its volume – there were no holey bits or heavier bits.

It was, to use the correct terminology, of "uniform density".

If that was the case then all the calculations proved that the gold foil, chosen because it could be made so thin, would be too insubstantial to stop the particles. The scientists thought that the gold atoms, lined up like a row of closely packed apples, would not resist the arrival of the helium particles – which would keep going and punch through.

Still, for the sake of scientific rigour, they tried it to see if the particles would bounce back, knowing that they wouldn't.

Mind you, devotion to science only goes so far. The younger Ernest's boss, the famous physicist Ernest Rutherford, had no intention of wasting his time sitting in a room waiting for something that could not happen. So Marsden sat there instead – and witnessed the impossible.

Most of the particles did indeed go through, but to Marsden's surprise he saw that every second or so a particle bounced back from the gold foil, creating a flash on a screen he had set up.

This made no sense. As Rutherford later said, "It was as if you fired a 15-inch shell at a piece of tissue paper and it came back and hit you."

Rutherford revised the calculations, and came to a startling conclusion.

A NEW ATOMIC MODEL

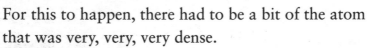

For this to happen, there had to be a bit of the atom that was very, very, very dense.

Rather than the gold sheet being pretty much the same density throughout, the mass of each atom must be concentrated in a small positively-charged ball in the centre – an extremely dense, extremely small, "nucleus".

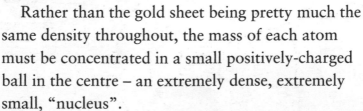

Only then would there be something heavy enough to make the particles bounce back.

Any particles that hit the empty space around the nucleus passed right through. All they had to contend with were negatively-charged and almost massless "electrons" that orbited the central core like planets in the solar system.

But the rare particle that collided with that core bounced right back and hit the screen.

The Ernests had learnt some important things: first, they had discovered what atoms looked like; second, they had shown once again that sometimes the most important questions in science are the ones you had assumed were already answered.

And third, the younger Ernest had learnt the timeless pleasure of making his boss look silly.

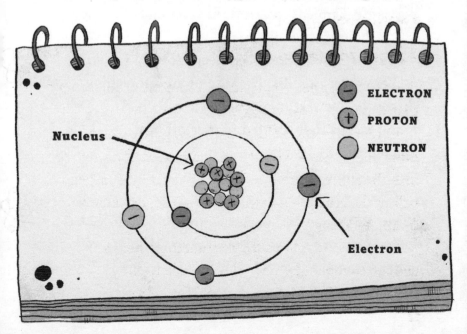

RADIATION

If you walked into the trendiest Manhattan bars of the 1920s you'd find the trendiest New Yorkers enjoying the latest trend: glow-in-the-dark drinks.

It wasn't just drinks that glowed in the dark back then. People could get glow-in-the-dark ink, glow-in-the-dark watches, glow-in-the-dark creams and, for those particularly delicate ailments, glow-in-the-dark suppositories.*

And, to be clear, these products weren't glow-in-the-dark in the way things are glow-in-the-dark today. When you crack a glow stick, for instance, you start a chemical reaction that continues for a few hours then fades away.

These, however, would keep glowing for years.

They were possible because of an astonishing discovery a few years earlier. Scientists had found metals that seemed to give off heat and light.

How could this be?

---

*If you don't know what a suppository is, **DON'T GOOGLE IT!** Suffice to say, there are two obvious orifices that can be used to give people medicine. One is your mouth. The other isn't.

ENERGY FROM NOWHERE

The discovery of these metals raised profound questions. What was the source of the light? Light is energy, so how were they making energy?

Was one of the most cherished ideas of Physics, that energy cannot be created out of nothing, incorrect?

Naturally, the public approached these materials with due reverence and awe, and the due care necessary for science that is not yet understood.

Only kidding. They made novelty drinks to be ingested in one end and novelty suppositories for the other.

For a brief time these radioactive materials weren't just exciting. They were seen as modern, health-giving and – when taken in drinks, advertisers eagerly explained – gave people energy.

Then, of course, people started to die.

NOT SO HEALTHY AFTER ALL

In a way, the advertisers' claims were correct, because radiation, which is what made the drinks glow, is indeed a form of energy.

However, this energy isn't created from nothing; it is created from the atoms inside the materials.

Remember the model of the atom a few pages back? In it an element was defined by the atomic number – the number of protons in its nucleus.

The number of neutrons, however, can vary. Uranium, for instance, always has 92 protons, but if it has 146 neutrons it is uranium-238, and if it has 143 it is uranium-235. These different versions of uranium are called **isotopes**.

Some isotopes just don't want to exist. They are unstable and fizzing, eager to be something else – something boring, that doesn't end up amazing people by glowing in cocktails.

The way they become something else is by changing their nucleus, by spewing out bits of themselves until they can calm down.

ALPHA RADIATION

For some of these materials, the quickest way to get their atoms to stabilize is known as **alpha decay:** they lose a particle that has two neutrons and two protons from their nucleus.

This particle, known as an **alpha particle,** skitters off and, because of its relatively big size, gets stopped quite quickly – by a sheet of paper or, if it is skittering from a suppository, by your bottom.

An alpha particle is a helium nucleus – it has two protons, two neutrons, but no electrons.

Just as isotopes are atoms with different numbers of neutrons, atoms with different numbers of electrons are ions. So an alpha particle is an ion of helium, with no electrons at all.

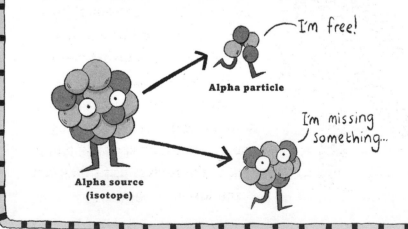

I'm free!

Alpha particle

I'm missing something...

Alpha source (isotope)

BETA DECAY

Other radioactive materials go through something called **beta decay**.

This is when a single electron, negatively-charged and nearly massless, spins out almost unnoticed from the nucleus – leaving behind one neutron that has been turned into a positively-charged proton.

Because electrons are smaller and sleeker than bumbling helium ions, beta radiation can go farther on its journey than the alpha radiation before being stopped.

Quite possibly, it will even escape your bottom.*

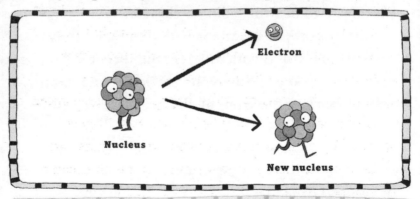

Electron

Nucleus

New nucleus

*A moderately thick sheet of metal will definitely stop it though, so it will get captured if you are wearing a suit of armour.

But if you fill your spare time wearing a suit of armour and using radioactive suppositories then you have bigger problems to deal with than the long-term effects of radiation.

GAMMA DECAY

Third and finally, there is gamma radiation. This is different to the others because it doesn't emit any particles. Instead the nucleus of the atom loses energy as an **electromagnetic proton**. And gamma radiation can travel through bottoms, through bottoms coated in suits of armour and in fact through a thick block of lead.

It matters how long radiation takes to stop – because when it does stop it causes damage. It steals electrons, or adds them where they shouldn't be.

When humans are exposed to beta or gamma radiation it careers through their skin and does damage to their organs. If this happens, you get cancer.

Alpha radiation is almost always safe. It gets stopped by skin, keeping your internal organs safe.

Of course, there is one instance in which it can't be stopped by skin – if it is already inside you. Then, instead, it is stopped by your internal organs. Which was why it was a very bad idea to put a major alpha source, an isotope of an element called radium, in a drink.

Unfortunately, no one told that to Eben Byers.

RADIATION SICKNESS

If only because they were so expensive, most people treated radioactive drinks as a novelty. But Mr Byers was extremely wealthy, and extremely addicted to RadiThor – the leading glow-in-the-dark drink of its time. He downed a bottle a day for three years.

Slowly, the radium accumulated in his system. It made its way into his bones, circulating around his body. There, particle by particle, the alpha radiation did its work. Holes appeared in his skull. His jaw fell off. He died a pretty unpleasant death.

Today, he is buried in a lead-lined coffin as, beneath the ground, the residue of those drinks continues to send radiation pinging out from his decaying bones.

It will keep doing so for many centuries yet.

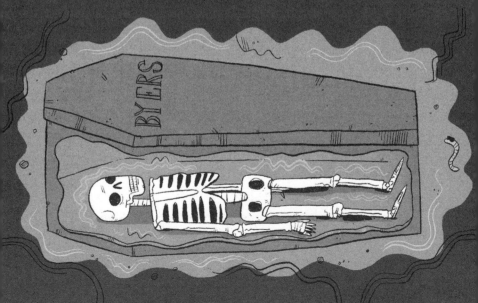

MARIE CURIE

The fact anyone knew about radium at all was thanks to Marie Curie.

Dr Curie is a member of the world's most elite club – she has two Nobel prizes. She also found two new elements, and coined the word radiation.

But, even so, her peers never let her forget she was a woman. She was refused entry to the French Academy of Sciences because of her sex.

Still, she had her revenge. The USA was more enlightened, and in 1921 the President invited her to the White House to present her with a gram of radium mined in America. The French, embarrassed she had not been honoured in her own country, offered her the Legion of Honour.

She turned it down.

HALF LIFE

The half life of a chunk of an isotope is how long it takes half of its atoms to decay. So if you have 1,000 atoms of radium, it's how long you have to wait for there to be 500 left.

The answer: 1,600 years. Which is why Marie

Curie's contaminated laboratory notes are still sealed in a lead box.

Some isotopes are so unstable they barely exist – their half lives are measured in million billionths of a second.

Some, such as tellurium-128, have been shown to decay so slowly that they have a half life a trillion times longer than the current age of the universe.

NUCLEAR POWER

What would you say upon witnessing the explosion of an apocalyptic super-weapon, the likes of which the world had never seen – and you had created it?

In 1945, scientists led by Robert Oppenheimer made an atomic bomb. It was able to harness the energy inside the atom's nucleus to produce a devastating explosion, so powerful that similar bombs would later destroy two cities in Japan.

Oppenheimer later said he was awed by his creation and, as he stood in front of the receding glow from the first nuclear test, he recalled words from Hindu scripture, "Now I am become Death, the destroyer of worlds."

Mind you, even if that really was what he was thinking, his brother Frank claimed his first spoken words were rather more boring: "It worked!"

HOW NUCLEAR FISSION WORKS

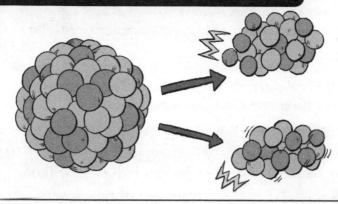

Every now and then an atom of uranium-235 splits into two smaller atoms, some neutrons and some energy.

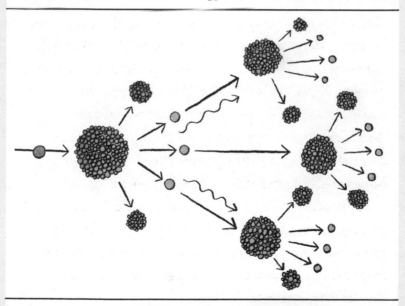

If these neutrons hit another atom of uranium-235, they make it split – and the same thing happens.

This means if you can get the atoms close enough together, so that the neutrons can't help but hit an atom, then you get a chain reaction.

This is what a nuclear bomb does. The first nuclear bomb ever used in war contained a gun that fired a lump of uranium into another lump of uranium.

When the two lumps violently combined, they made something dense enough for a nuclear chain reaction, releasing a lot of neutrons, a lot smaller atoms and a heck of a lot of energy.

Later, even more devastating bombs were developed. Instead of just splitting atoms apart they also joined others together in what is called a **FUSION REACTION**. This made even more energy.

Einstein discovered there was an equation that explained all of this. It is probably the most famous equation in the world:

This equation relates energy to mass. It is the reason the Sun can project energy and Vladimir Putin, say, can project power. It shows that a very small change in mass, for instance in nuclear reactions, can lead to a vast amount of energy.

Under extremely high temperatures and pressures – for instance, inside the Sun or a nuclear bomb – hydrogen nuclei can fuse together to make helium.

When they do, the mass of the helium atom is ever so slightly less than that of the hydrogen ones that made it – that difference is recorded in the equation as "m".

To realize just what a large amount of energy a small amount of mass can make, you need to understand how big "c" is.

In Physics, "c" means the speed of light. Light covers 300,000 kilometres in a second – travelling roughly seven and a half times around the world. So "c squared" is an unimaginably large number, multiplied by itself.

All of which means that not very much mass can, in the case of the Sun, warm our Earth, grow our crops and sustain life.

Or alternatively, put to other uses, annihilate it.

IN SHORT: If it glows, don't put it inside you.

WHAT YOU NEED TO KNOW:

- **Atoms** can be thought of as very, very dense cores containing **neutrons** and **protons**, that are surrounded by the orbits of almost massless **electrons**.

- An **element** is defined by the number of protons its atoms have – but the number of neutrons can change. This means there can be different versions of an element, with different masses. These are called **isotopes**.

- If isotopes are elements with differing numbers of neutrons, **ions** are elements with differing numbers of electrons.

- Some atoms are **radioactive**, which means they are unstable and want to decay.

- They can do this through **alpha decay**, in which they emit a helium nucleus; through **beta decay**, in which an electron is emitted and a neutron turns into a proton; or through **gamma decay**, in which they emit energy.

- **Alpha radiation** causes the most damage, but is the easiest to stop. **Gamma radiation** causes the least, but is the hardest to stop. **Beta** is in between.

- Nuclear power involves breaking up atoms (**fission**) or joining them together (**fusion**) to turn mass into energy.

WHAT YOU DON'T NEED TO KNOW, BUT MIGHT LIKE TO: *SCHRÖDINGER'S CAT*

Ah, that's sweet.

What?

The fact that Schrödinger had a cat. It's nice to know that world-famous physicists are still like us.

He didn't have a cat, it only existed in a thought experiment.

Well, it's lovely that he was still thinking about having a cat then. What was he planning to do with it?

Put it in a box with a vial of poison.

Ah. May I ask why?

To make a point about the paradoxical nature of reality, and the futility of dividing the macro from the micro.

Good good. And cats have to die for this?

Actually no. The point was that the cat was neither alive nor dead. It both lost one of its nine lives, and didn't.

And he thought this was ... logical?

No, he thought it was ludicrous.

At least we can agree on that.
Why did he make it then?

In the early twentieth century a new form of Physics emerged called quantum mechanics.

It took the model of atoms and particles that Rutherford created, and said that it was not quite right.

Particles such as electrons did not exist in one place as Rutherford thought. Instead, they were both waves and particles – existing as a probabilistic smear across space.

Eh?

One of the simplest ways of imagining it is that they exist in lots of places at the same time.

I won't ask what the more complex ways are. How come things, y'know, appear to be in one place?

When you observe something, it seems to fix its position. The act of seeing something in a place, puts it in that place.

That's ridiculous. Please tell me that's ridiculous.

Schrödinger certainly thought it was ... problematic.

Some physicists sought to explain it by saying that quantum mechanics only applied to very small things, so in our world of big things the craziness doesn't matter.

Schrödinger said you can't do that – and that's where the cat (which is, for these purposes, a "big thing") comes in.

Go on.

Imagine you put a cat in a box with a very, very small amount of a radioactive substance, and a radiation detector linked to a vial of poison.

Why would I do this?

Because cats are evil and hate you and you really should get a dog.

Only kidding. Because it is a way of linking something small – a single atom of a radioactive material – to something big, a cat.

If an atom of the radioactive substance decays, it triggers the detector that releases the poison and kills the cat. Otherwise, the cat lives.

Seems simple enough.

It's not. Until the box is opened, the atom has not been observed so, according to some interpretations of quantum mechanics, it has both decayed and not decayed.

As a consequence, the cat is both alive and dead.

So quantum mechanics shows cats can be both alive and not alive?

No. It is patently obvious that a cat cannot be simultaneously alive and dead.

The mortality or otherwise of cats is one of those rare points on which physicists are happy to listen to biologists.

Does this mean quantum mechanics is wrong?

Absolutely not. It is an amazing theory that explains much of the world.

But, as the cat shows, it cannot be the whole story. If a theory says a cat both lives and doesn't live, we need to re-examine the Physics rather than the feline.

To summarize: don't give physicists pets.

CHAPTER 4

ELECTRICITY

INTRODUCTION
ELECTRICITY

IN THIS CHAPTER YOU WILL LEARN ABOUT:

- Electricity as the movement of electrons
- Current and voltage
- Resistance
- AC and DC
- Static electricity

BEFORE YOU READ THIS CHAPTER:

For the ancients, electricity was a mysterious force controlled by gods. Its awesome power came in thunderbolts flung down by Zeus, or in the rages of a hammer-wielding Thor.

We now know it is, in some ways, rather less exciting. Of the three particles that make up an atom – the neutron, proton and electron, described in Chapter Three – the electron seems the least significant. Almost massless, it whizzes around in a void, barely existing at all.

But it is, in its own way, just as important.

When electrons move – not in an atom, but between them – astonishing things happen.

This is why our ancestors were, perhaps, right to think of electricity that way. Because after humans eventually understood and tamed the electron, it gave us powers that even Zeus would have found impressive...

CURRENT

One day in 1746, 200 monks briefly flinched, cried out in pain, and – spread out in a circle half a kilometre wide – spasmed.

Watching this conga line of convulsing clergy, their fellow monk Jean-Antoine Nollet smiled. For he was the one who had electrified them, and he was very pleased indeed.

"It is singular," he later wrote, "to see the multitude of different gestures, and to hear the instantaneous exclamation of those surprised by the shock!"

The key word in that sentence, and the reason Nollet was so pleased, is "instantaneous".

JEAN-ANTOINE NOLLET

THE SPEED OF CURRENT

The question for Nollet was, how long would it take for the electricity to travel around the circle? The answer, he knew, would come in their screams of pain.

Would each monk receive a jolt in turn – crying out one after the other like an echo bouncing around the monastery's cloisters? Or would they call out in unison – a cacophony of 200 cries and shouts worthy of the torments of hell they were all warned about in daily sermons?

Nollet was in the monastery that day to answer a debate about electricity.

History does not record how well informed the monks were about electricity. But after Nollet made them stand in a big circle, connected them to each other using lengths of wire, then switched on a really big battery, they probably got the idea quite fast.

That day, as he saw the circle of twitching monks, Nollet had his answer: hellish cacophony it was. The charge moved, he said, instantaneously – producing no discernible difference between the first monk and the last.

And so, through the brief pain of 200 confused and cross monks, we got closer to understanding one of the most mysterious phenomena in our daily lives – electricity.

In the centuries since, we have slowly worked out what was causing the brothers of that Carthusian abbey such inconvenience.

It was moving electrons.

THE NATURE OF CURRENT

Electrons move all the time, spinning around the nuclei of atoms. But when they move in an organized, systematic way, we call that **electric current**. And current comes about thanks to something else – **voltage**.

BUT WHAT IF I'M NOT USING A BATTERY?

With the electricity that comes out of plugs in the wall, the water analogy still works – but the circuit

A DIGRESSION ... THE WATER ANALOGY

Before we get on to what is going on with the monks, we need to properly understand electricity. One of the easiest ways to do that is to compare it to water.

1 A BATTERY is like a pump, pulling electrons up to a reservoir.

2 The VOLTAGE, or POTENTIAL DIFFERENCE, in this analogy is the height of the reservoir.

In a battery what this actually means is that it has pulled lots of electrons to one side of it where, like water held up high, they desperately want to flow back.

Voltage is what makes the electrons want to move.

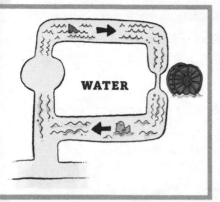

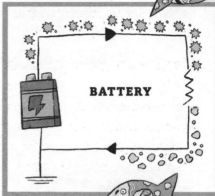

3 A RESISTOR is where the energy of the electrons is transferred to other stores – like a waterwheel being turned by a river. Afterwards, just as with a river that is slowed by moving a wheel, the electrons have less energy.

4 The CURRENT in electricity is the number of electrons flowing – in the same way as the current in water is the amount of water flowing.

5 Sometimes, a river splits in two then rejoins. Circuits are the same.

The current divides between the two, with more current going down the easier route (in the case of water, the wider one, in the case of electricity, the one with least resistance).

Each parcel of water, and electrons, carries the same energy into its branch. This is what happens in what is called a PARALLEL CIRCUIT.

looks a bit different.

Instead of having a battery pumping up electrons, there is a **generator** – moving them first one way then another. It is a bit like a paddle swishing to and fro very fast.

Now let us return to the monks, as they nervously link up awaiting Nollet's next scheme.

Nollet's battery had built up a big charge – like a

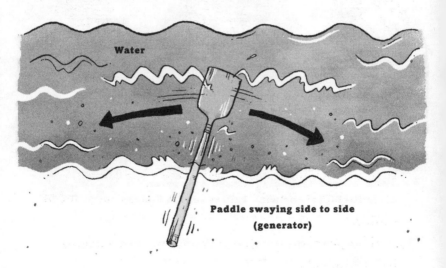

Water

Paddle swaying side to side
(generator)

reservoir high on a mountain. Like all batteries, the electrons in it wanted to move back to the other side of the battery, but couldn't.

To move, they needed to go the long way instead – through all the monks holding hands.
BUT HOW DID THEY MOVE?

Given a choice, electrons prefer to move in metal wires rather than monks.

They move around by bouncing from atom to atom. So one electron will bounce into the first atom and displace one of its electrons, which will in turn bounce into the second atom – and so on.

But that is not all that is needed to make a monk dance.

The problem for the electrons is, they have to have somewhere to go.

It's all very well saying that an electron from the

ELECTRONS IN A WIRE

battery will push out an electron in the first atom of the wire, which will push one out in the second atom, then the third then the fourth, etc.

But that all fails if there is nowhere for the last electron to go. Because if that happens there will just be an electron traffic jam.

The answer, Nollet knew, was to connect the wire in a circle, or circuit. Then the last electron could go into the battery, get pumped to the other side, and begin the journey again.

The volume of electrons doing this is called the **current**.

But a circuit just made of wire, without even a solitary monk in it, is a sad circuit.

With nothing to slow them down, the electrons whizz around, a lot of current comes out of the battery, and it gets very hot indeed. This is called a

short circuit, and it's not very safe.

That is why you need a resistor. A resistor is something that the electrons have to work to get through. Sometimes they do this by making heat – that is what an electric heater is.

Sometimes they do it by making light – that is what a lightbulb is.

And sometimes if you choose a very specialist resistor, the kind, say, that is soft, squidgy and wears a cassock, they make a screaming sound.

VERY SPEEDY, AND ALSO VERY SLOW

Electricity seems to flow instantaneously, but individual electrons move very slowly. In a typical copper wire attached to a battery, it takes about three minutes for an electron to move a centimetre.

The reason a light goes on the instant you flick the switch is not because each electron moves fast. It's because each electron is part of a chain, shoving the next onwards.

LIGHTNING ROD

In later life Roy Sullivan, a US park ranger, became known as "Human Lightning Rod". He was hit seven times by lightning – yet miraculously survived.

The last time he was hit by lightning, his luck got even worse. He came to, with his hair on fire, to see that a bear was stealing his food.

What he was experiencing was an extreme form of static electricity. Ordinarily you experience static electricity when, say, you rub a balloon on your jumper and transfer some electrons – which gives it charge that means it can stick on the wall.

If a lot more electrons accumulate, in a cloud for instance, then that is a larger-scale form of static electricity – and also a signal that Sullivan was about to have a bad day.

Once, he admitted he felt cursed. "I can be standing in a crowd of people, but it'll hit me. I'm just allergic to lightning," he said, glumly.

His friends certainly agreed – they sensibly took to avoiding him during storms.

THE CURRENT WARS

In 1888, two dozen of New York's most distinguished residents gathered to watch a dog drink some water.

But it refused. Whenever it was pulled towards the bowl, it would back away. Once, it resisted so violently it managed to break its lead.

Eventually, terrified, it tried to leap over the bowl, and a single foot splashed in the water. It was cnough.

"There was a quick contortion," a journalist wrote, "and the little cur dog fell dead."

Thomas Edison, the American inventor, had wired up that bowl of water to 1,500 volts of electricity.

Over the years Edison and his compatriots would kill many other dogs, as well as cats, calves and a horse.

The reason they did this was that they wanted to show that a particular kind of electricity is bad – and the reason they wanted to do that was that Edison had made a bad bet.

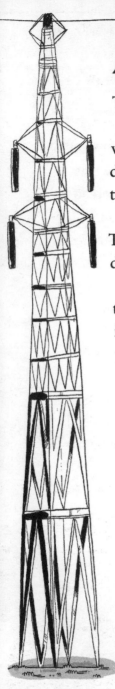

AC AND DC

There are two types of electricity supply.

The first is **direct current** (DC). This is where the current always flows in the same direction – it is what comes out of batteries today.

The second is **alternating current** (AC). This is where the current continually changes direction, and it is what comes out of plugs.

The advantage of alternating current is that its form can be easily changed. When it is in electricity pylons it can be very high voltage – with lots of electrical potential – and low current, with not many electrons.

The lower the current, the less power is lost in the wire – so it can travel further cheaper.

Then when it arrives at your home it can be converted back to low voltage and high current.

Unfortunately for Edison, his company supplied direct current – and because of the problem of power loss, the electricity he supplied was a lot more expensive than his AC competitor, a man called George Westinghouse.

If he could not make electricity cheaper than Westinghouse, then Edison was going to show he could make electricity safer. He did this by deciding to prove how dangerous AC was and using it to fry animals.

His argument was half right: 1,500 V of AC in a water bowl is indeed a pretty unpleasant surprise for a thirsty dog – but it is no more lethal than 1,500 V of DC.

THE BATTLE FOR SUPREMACY

The "Current War", as Edison's battle with Westinghouse would be known, got sillier before it got sensible.

There was, for instance, a serious attempt by the DC camp to define being killed by an electric shock as not "electrocution" but as "being Westinghoused".

Then there was the duel. One of Edison's associates wrote a letter challenging Westinghouse to an electrocution contest. Each would be wired up to their favoured form of current, and the voltage would slowly be increased. The last to give up would be declared the victor.

EDISON

WESTINGHOUSE

Westinghouse declined.

And ultimately, Edison lost the only duel that mattered: the contest to supply the world's electricity. Because even the smouldering and charred remains of a horse aren't able to compete with economics.

AC was simply better.

IN SHORT: Electricity: good news for humanity, bad news for monks.

WHAT YOU NEED TO KNOW:

- **Electricity** is what happens when electrons move.
- We measure electricity using **current** and **voltage**.
- Current is the rate of flow of electrons, voltage is what is needed to make the electrons flow.
- **Resistance** – from light bulbs, heaters or monks – makes it harder for current to flow.
- There are two types of electricity: **AC**, which switches direction all the time and comes from your plug, and **DC**, which always flows in the same direction and comes from batteries.
- Both kinds need a **circuit** to flow.
- There is also **static electricity**, which comes from an electron imbalance between two objects – such as balloons and jumpers, or Roy Sullivan and clouds.

WHAT YOU DON'T NEED TO KNOW, BUT MIGHT LIKE TO:
SEMICONDUCTORS

I know these, they're like superconductors but more rubbish.

Absolutely not. Semiconductors are possibly the most important invention of the twentieth century.

So what does the "semi" bit mean then?

That they are less good at conducting.

Right. I refer you to my first point.

Sometimes, though, a less good conductor is exactly what you want. Particularly when you want to use electricity to solve problems.

I always use electricity to solve problems. Like making light, and cooking my dinner.

I meant problems more along the lines of "What will the weather be like tomorrow?" or "Who is big on Instagram at the moment?"

For that, you need a semiconductor – specifically, silicon.

Ah, that's different. So how does silicon help you waste a bus journey looking at cat memes – I mean, how does silicon help you predict the weather?

Bear with me on this, it's complicated.

Silicon is only just able to conduct electricity. It forms a really strong lattice, where each atom is joined to four others and no electrons are have anywhere to move.

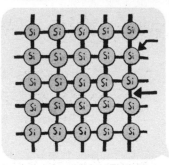

But if you mix it with a tiny bit of an impurity, such as phosphorus, then that changes. Phosphorus has five electrons in its outer layer, which means that if you put it into the lattice there is one left free to roam. This is called N-type silicon.

If you mix it instead with gallium, which has just three electrons, there is a hole for electrons to roam into. It is called P-type silicon. Both are good conductors.

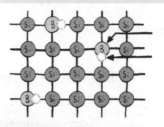

Great, so you've turned a bad conductor into a good conductor in two different ways. Why not just start with a good conductor?

Because the magic happens when you join the two together.

Put a bit of N-silicon next to a bit of P-silicon and you get something called a diode. It will only let electricity pass one way.

I'm still not seeing the use.

And what do you think then happens though if you make a P-silicon sandwich: NPN? Or an N-silicon sandwich, PNP?

Well, if an NP lets it go one way, and PN lets it go another, then I guess NPN stops it completely?

Exactly!

Right...

But here's the clever bit. If you have an NPN or PNP sandwich and you pass a small current through the middle, then it will let current through. It's a switch – a switch you can make really, really small, and control really precisely.

Why do I want small and precise switches?

Because you can think of them as being "1" when closed and "0" when open... Is this ringing any bells?

Wait, is that binary?

Yes, computer language. And you can join the switches together in clever ways to make use of that. You could, for instance, make an "AND gate", which takes in two inputs and only passes a current if both are "on".

Or an "OR gate", which also takes in two inputs and passes a current if either of them is on.

If a current passes, in binary it's a "1" if it doesn't, it's a "0".

This still seems a long way from giving people mobile phones that can access the entirety of the world's information, but which they actually use to browse Instagram.

It is. About 75 years, in fact. But in the 1950s, having a few of these "logic gates" meant that computers could perform calculations far faster and far more accurately than a human being.

Having millions of them meant they could attempt to predict the weather, with the first primitive supercomputers.

And having billions meant you could waste the best years of your life trying to work out if celebrities are Photoshopping their selfies?

You've got it.

CHAPTER 5

NEWTON

INTRODUCTION
NEWTON

IN THIS CHAPTER YOU WILL LEARN ABOUT:

- Newton's Laws of Motion
- Speed, velocity and acceleration
- Vectors and scalars
- Weight and mass
- Hooke's law
- Moments and levers

What goes up must come down... Every action has an equal and opposite reaction... If something is heading in one direction, it will only start heading in another if you apply a force...

Newton's work might seem a bit obvious now, but at the time it was a revelation. With his laws of motion he saw, more clearly than any person who came before, that the universe obeyed rules.

The same rules that describe how an apple drops, how a cannonball flies and how two snooker balls collide also describe how planets, stars and galaxies move.

He was not alone – others helped, in our understanding of how objects moved. This chapter also includes the theories first outlined by Archimedes, looking at levers and moments, and the theories of Hooke, who considered how forces could stretch things.

But Newton's contribution was the greatest. He saw a universe in an apple. He arrived into a world that believed in magic, and left behind a world that understood order.

NEWTON

One day in the 1660s, a young scientist decided to find out how the eye worked. As all tinkerers know, the first step to investigating something is to poke it.

Most people don't like you poking their eyes though. So Isaac Newton went to the only person he knew would say yes: himself.

He got a big needle and, in his own words, "put it betwixt my eye and bone as neare to [the] backside of my eye as I could." Then he gave it a good wiggle.

He was most satisfied with the results. "There appeared severall white darke & coloured circles," he wrote in his notebook – helpfully labelling them on a diagram.

Newton would go on to revolutionize the study of optics, in a very small part thanks to this experiment.

But most people would forget about all that work, given he also revolutionized the study of mathematics, astronomy and the motion of objects.

Newton was a man who was not afraid to undertake sacrifices for his work. He was also, it has to be said, a little bit odd. But maybe that's what it requires to, in his words, see further by standing on the shoulders of giants.

Consider a football flying through the air, an iPhone dropping to the ground, a car turning a corner. It takes an unusual mind to think that three simple rules can explain the motion of all these objects.

And more, it takes an extraordinary mind to show, as Newton did with calculus, that you can divide the world into infinitesimally small sections and end up with one of the most powerful tools in mathematics.

And it probably takes a mind that already believes a bit in magic to derive from all this the law of gravity – which only made sense at the time if you assumed planets and stars could exert forces instantaneously over millions of miles without touching each other.

But it was when Newton turned to proper magic that things got really weird.

He spent years trying to find the "Philosopher's Stone", the elixir of life that he believed could also convert base metals into gold.

At the same time, he conducted close textual analysis of the Bible to try to find out all that he could about the end of the world (2060 may be a key date, in case you were wondering).

Newton heralded the arrival of the modern world. Perhaps he is best understood, as the economist John Maynard Keynes would later put it, as "not the first of the age of reason, but the last of the magicians."

NEWTON'S PAWS OF MOTION

Newton had a dog called Diamond. Reputedly, one day it knocked over a candle and set fire to 20 years' worth of manuscripts. Newton exclaimed, "O Diamond, Diamond, thou little knowest the mischief thou hast done." But, so the story goes, he did forgive her and give her a hug.

> **NEWTON'S LAWS OF MOTION**
>
> - **First Law:** An object stays doing what it is doing – staying still, or moving at a steady speed in a straight line – unless there is an external force.
> - **Second Law:** The acceleration of an object is proportional to the force applied.
> - **Third Law:** Every action has an equal and opposite reaction.

The laws of motion are the bit of Newton that doesn't involve apples. It's also the bit you are most likely to have actually heard of.

This is the bit that says that every action has an equal and opposite reaction. Or: if you drive into a concrete wall with a force of X, that wall repays by hitting you in turn with a force of minus X.

That's the third law, and not only is it the reason why concrete walls hurt, it is also why rockets fly. Most people think they move because they are pushing off on something – the air, say, or the ground.

In 1919 Dr Robert Goddard proposed, in a paper titled "A Method of Reaching Extreme Altitudes", using rockets to get into space.

The New York Times was scornful of this idea – in space, it said, there is nothing to push against.

"Professor Goddard does not know the relation of action and reaction, and of the need to have something better than a vacuum against which to react," the paper wrote. They said that he lacked "the knowledge ladled out daily in high schools".

Actually high schools teach quite the opposite.

Rockets don't push on anything – they throw gas very fast in one direction, and are propelled with the same momentum in the opposite direction. If you sit in a shopping trolley and throw baked bean cans out of it you will achieve the same effect.

You may even become turbocharged by supermarket security guiding you to the exit.

THE SECOND AND FIRST LAW

That was just the third law, the other laws are equally crucial. Newton's first law states that a body stays in motion unless acted upon by an outside force. Such as, say, a car hitting a wall.

The second law describes what happens when that wall arrives. It says that how fast you slow down (**acceleration**, or **deceleration** in this case), depends on the mass of the object and force applied.

This is better known by the equation $\mathbf{F = ma}$.

In car-and-concrete-wall terms, this means that the more your front wheel can crumple the more time it takes to stop, hence the slower the deceleration – and the smaller the force you have to deal with in subsequent whiplash claims.

And what of that chap Goddard? He later had a NASA space centre named after him, and *The New York Times* (much) later published a correction... "Further investigation and experimentation have confirmed the findings of Isaac Newton."

NEWTON'S FIRST LAW

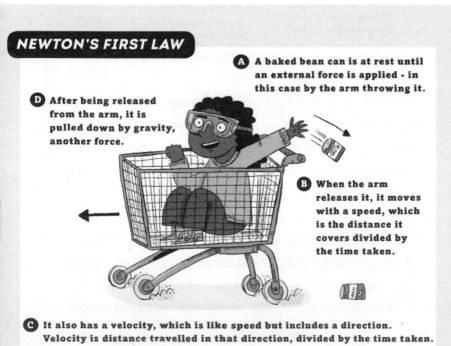

A A baked bean can is at rest until an external force is applied - in this case by the arm throwing it.

D After being released from the arm, it is pulled down by gravity, another force.

B When the arm releases it, it moves with a speed, which is the distance it covers divided by the time taken.

C It also has a velocity, which is like speed but includes a direction. Velocity is distance travelled in that direction, divided by the time taken.

A The mass of a baked bean can multiplied by its acceleration when thrown is the same as the force applied.

B Acceleration is the rate at which velocity changes. In this case the mass of the can is 0.5kg, the acceleration is 100m/s², and so the force must have been 50N - a highly respectable baked bean can throw.

C Things that don't have a direction, like speed (and mass and temperature) are scalar quantities. Things that do have direction are vector.

The trolley's scalar values are:

Mass: 100kg
Speed: still not very fast, but you're flinging out cans as fast as you can
Temperature: 20°C, but hotting up as you see a security guard approach

VECTOR AND SCALAR

Weight, a vector, is different from mass, a scalar. That is why an astronaut can weigh nothing in space, but still have exactly the same mass. Weight only happens with gravity too, and it is the gravity that gives it direction.

On the surface of the Earth, acceleration due to gravity is 9.8m/s. So the weight of a 100kg person is 100x9.8 Newtons, or 980 Newtons, in a downward direction.

NEWTON'S THIRD LAW

E When it hits the ground it stops. Why? For the same reason the trolley also isn't pulled through the ground. The ground pushes back with an equal and opposite contact force – Newton's third law again.

A Every action, including baked bean-related ones, has an equal and opposite reaction.

B So if the can is thrown with a 50N force in one direction, the trolley is propelled with a 50N force in the other.

F = 50N
Mass = 100kg
So acceleration = 0.5m/s²

D Once released, the can is accelerated down by gravity, falling at 9.8m/s².

C You would have to throw a lot of cans to go fast, particularly as friction in the wheels will cause some kinetic energy (see Chapter Two) to be lost as heat, slowing it down.

MOMENTUM

A Let's assume somehow that you throw enough cans to get a good velocity, of 10m/s. Your momentum is mass times velocity – in this case 100x10, or 1000kgm/s.

B Momentum is one of those quantities that is conserved. If you hit another stationary trolley of 100kg and you both continue along together, then total momentum must be the same. Since the combined mass of the two trolleys is 200kg, the combined velocity must halve to 5m/s.

C If you then hit a 100kg security guard as well, it will drop again to 3.33m/s. Until, that is, the security guard applies a new force to the system – and pushes you out the door.

A FISHY TALE

As far as Newton was concerned, his laws of motion had one great flaw: they were too easy to understand. He was worried this would mean that normal people might read them – a truly alarming prospect. To ensure this terrifying scenario never came to pass, when he wrote them in a book he laboured to make it as needlessly complex as possible – "to avoid," he explained, "being baited by little smatterers in mathematics."

He was almost too successful at avoiding the smatterers. He wanted to publish it with the Royal Society, a scientific institution still going today. Unfortunately, they had just lost a lot of money publishing a book called *The History of Fishes*.

Actual sales were so far below expected that they had taken to paying their staff in fish books.

The Society reasoned, sensibly, that if they couldn't flog a book about fish they were unlikely to do better with a book that had the express purpose of not making sense.

Only a private benefactor saved him – providing the money to publish his masterwork, known today as the *Principia*.

The book was simultaneously a monument to the soaring majesty of the human mind, and – in its sheer, pointless tedium – a monument to its pettiness.

Still, at least it outsold the fish book.

MOMENTS AND LEVERS

As a great pile of steaming dung flew towards the walls of Karlštejn Castle, did the castle's defenders stop to ponder the theory of turning forces and moments?

As it reached the top of its arc, a vast stinky globule of flying poo hanging apparently motionless against the medieval sky of Bohemia, did they take time to consider the exquisite simplicity of the trebuchet's balance of forces?

Probably not. They were likely more keen not to be standing wherever it was about to go splat.

But even if they did not consider the theory of turning moments, the "trebuchet" – a siege

117

machine that in 1422 was deployed to fill Karlštejn Castle with 2,000 carriage-loads of poo – could not work without it.

The Chinese were the first to develop a trebuchet, using it to fling burning logs at enemies in the fourth century BCE. The Mongol Empire swept through Asia thanks to the trebuchet's mighty power – bringing the Black Death with them as they launched diseased corpses into besieged towns.

And in 1422, the besiegers of Karlštejn Castle decided to make life unpleasant for its defenders by using a trebuchet to turn their home into a disease-ridden cesspool.

The trebuchet is not a catapult. It doesn't use tension to bend wood, like a bow. It doesn't even have elastic.

The reason it was so successful that is it was far simpler than that. It was just a large wooden arm that could swing on a pivot. On the short end was a big heavy weight, on the other end was whatever it was you wanted to fling – whether diseased bodies, poo or rocks.

How do you get the weights right, to ensure the vanquishing of your foes? You calculate the turning moments.

A moment is not something real. It is a useful mathematical tool to help us calculate how things with pivots (such as trebuchets, wheelbarrows and levers) move. If you have a force pushing up or down on a beam, the moment is the force multiplied by the distance from the pivot that the force is applied.

So if the big weight is 1m from the pivot and is 1,000 Newtons, its turning moment is 1,000 Newton-metres.

If the little weight (of poo) is 5m from the pivot and is 200 Newtons, its moment is also 1,000 Nm. This means the trebuchet doesn't move — the total moment is 1,000 minus 1,000.

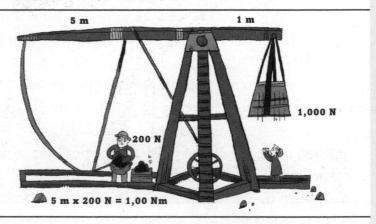

If the fetid pile of poo-ammunition is instead 400 Newtons, its moment is 2,000 Nm. So the trebuchet turns, but in the wrong way — with a net moment of 1,000 Nm.

To get the poo to fling into the faces of your enemies then, you either need less of it – the coward's way out – or a heavier weight at the other end. 2,000 Newtons should do it:

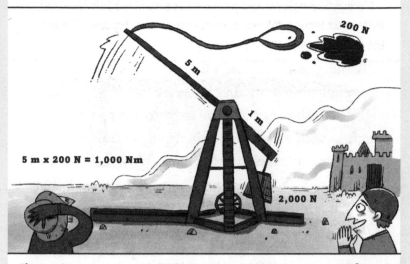

5 m x 200 N = 1,000 Nm

200 N

5 m

1 m

2,000 N

The turning moment now is 2,000 Nm minus 1,000 Nm – a very satisfactory 1,000 Nm that easily gets your pile of poo over the walls. Hurrah!

LEVERS

"Give me a place to stand," said the Greek mathematician Archimedes, "and with a lever I will move the Earth."

Turning moments are not only used to make big weights move smaller weights fast – as in a trebuchet. They can also be used to make little weights (such as Greek mathematicians) move bigger weights (such as planets) slowly.

A force applied far from the pivot can, using the same equations, move even very heavy things close to the pivot.

This is called a **lever,** and it is the principle behind pliers, wheelbarrows and crowbars – and a lot else besides.

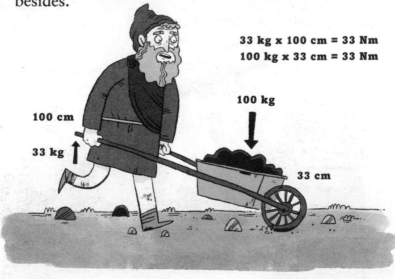

33 kg x 100 cm = 33 Nm
100 kg x 33 cm = 33 Nm

100 kg

100 cm

33 kg

33 cm

HOOKE

There are no known pictures of Robert Hooke, and historians think they know why: Newton destroyed them.

Newton and Hooke were two scientists who hated each other. They first fell out over light – one of them thought it was a wave, the other a particle. Then they fell out over gravity: Hooke claimed that Newton did not give him enough credit for his contributions.

By the time of Hooke's death, he was clinging on as president of the Royal Society simply to deny Newton the position. Unfortunately for him, when Newton did take over, the first thing he did was go about erasing his predecessor's reputation – and, quite possibly, his portraits too.

It can never be proved with certainty but, as one scholar put it, he had "motive, means and opportunity".

Or, as another scholar said of Hooke's official Royal Society portrait, "I would not have trusted Newton with a box of matches anywhere near it."

But while you can destroy an oil painting, you can't destroy a theory. So Hooke's science lives on; in particular, "Hooke's law".

Hooke said that if you have a spring, the amount it extends is proportional to the force applied. So if you dangle 100 g on the end of it, it extends twice as far as if you dangle 50 g.

IN SHORT: Newton: great man, with great theories – but you wouldn't want him round for dinner.

WHAT YOU NEED TO KNOW:

- **Newton's Laws of Motion** govern the movement of objects. They are:
  1. An object keeps going in the same direction or stays still until you apply a force to it.
  2. Acceleration is proportional to the force applied.
  3. Every action has an equal and opposite reaction.
- **Speed** is distance covered divided by the time taken.
- **Velocity** is like speed but it also has direction. It is displacement – a term for distance travelled along with its direction – divided by the time taken.
- **Acceleration** is the rate of change of velocity.
- **Scalar quantities** are things like **temperature**, **speed** and **mass**, which don't have a direction.
- **Vector quantities** – such as acceleration and force – *do* have a direction they act in.
- The **momentum** of an object is its mass times its velocity, and momentum is conserved.
- **Hooke's Law** states that the extension of an elastic spring is proportional to the force applied.
- **Turning moments** help you work out what happens on – among other things – seesaws, levers and trebuchets. The turning moment of a rigid bar is the distance to the pivot times the force applied.

WHAT YOU DON'T NEED TO KNOW, BUT MIGHT LIKE TO:
SPECIAL RELATIVITY

What else do I need to know about Newton's laws?

Everything I just told you is wrong.

Eh?

In 1905 Einstein came along and described a new theory that displaced Newton's. It was called special relativity.

What's so special about it?

It is one of the most beautiful works of the human mind: a theory, based largely on thought experiments, that swept in a grand new age of scientific discovery.

No, what I mean is, why is it called special relativity?

Because it does not take gravity into account. And ignoring gravity, in Physics, is pretty special.

Doesn't sound too special to me.

It was a huge leap. It completely changed our view of Physics.

To the Victorians, Physics had seemed easy. Building on the work of Newton and Galileo, they had imagined a neatly ordered universe.

Theirs was a Physics where if I run, say, at 10mph and bowl a ball at 40mph, the ball has a speed of 50mph.

So how did special relativity change this?

Einstein came along and said, actually, that's not quite right. The properties of the ball really depend on if you're the bowler, the batsman ... or the ball.

To the first two, the ball seems to shrink in flight, and time goes less rapidly.

The batsman and bowler see odd things happening – while from the ball's point of view, everything's fine.

Why would this happen?

First, you need to know how Einstein came up with this idea. Its premise is deceptively simple: the laws of Physics are the same for everyone, however they move relative to each other.

Imagine you are in a train, with a tape measure and a newspaper. It would be odd if the newspaper measured longer to you when you were moving than when stopped.

And it doesn't: the laws are the same. So far, so simple.

What have rulers and newspapers got to do with the speed of light?

Some physical laws rely on the speed of light. For them to be the same in or out of your train, light speed also has to be the same.

So why does this make cricket balls shrink?

It doesn't, the point is … look, this is really hard stuff.

The ball appears to shrink – or, rather, its apparent size depends on who is looking at it, and how fast they are relative to it.

Anyway, assume the ball is being thrown towards the stadium lights. It is going at 50mph...

I thought you said...

Like I said, it is going at approximately 50mph. So how fast does the light hit it?

50mph, plus the speed of light?

No. It hits it at the speed of light. The same light also hits the bowler at the speed of light.

Even if the bowler ran towards the stadium lights at half the speed of light, the closing speed would still be the speed of light.

The only way this can happen is if time and distance, rather than being fixed quantities, are variable.

So Einstein said that as things get faster they also get shorter, and experience a slowing down of time?

Not exactly. He said they appear to do so to observers, such as the bowler. As far as the ball is concerned, everything is normal.

Who's right?

Both. Quantities such as distance and time depend on the person viewing them.

What if you go faster than the speed of light?

You can't. The resulting equations imply that to reach it would require an infinite amount of energy. If you did somehow find that much energy, you would appear to shrink to nothing.

So what does all this mean for non-scientists?

Mainly, that most people can't understand most Physics any more.

CHAPTER 6

WAVES

INTRODUCTION
WAVES

IN THIS CHAPTER YOU WILL LEARN ABOUT:

- Waves and the transfer of energy
- Reflection and refraction
- Lenses
- The electromagnetic spectrum
- Black body radiation

Waves are the universe's method of transferring energy. They are the vibrations that travel through matter, or the light that takes heat from the Sun to Earth.

This chapter is about how they move and how they spread.

To understand waves, you need to understand **energy** (see Chapter 2). But waves are so much more than just energy on the move: they are how humans experience the world.

The shiver in your spine when you hear Martin Luther King's "I Have a Dream" speech, the joy you feel when you see a flower in spring, the happiness you experience when your favourite band plays?

All occur for no other reason than that your brain has evolved to send particular signals in response to particular waves.

A SEISMIC GOAL

Sometimes, football teams cause earthquakes.
Quite literally.

In the Institute of Earth Sciences, a mile from
Barcelona's main football stadium, there is a
machine that tells the scientists when there has
been a goal.

It is not sound it measures, though. The cheer
of the crowd has long since faded, reduced to
undetectable levels, before reaching the machine.
Instead it is vibrations, travelling in the ground, that
cause its needle to jump.

As the crowd leaps to its feet in celebration,
100,000 pairs of feet pound the ground as one. As
they sit down again, 100,000 bottoms send another
slightly more cushioned shock through the stadium's
foundations.

And a few seconds later, the ripples from those
feet and bottoms, spreading out through the
ground, are registered at the Institute.

The scientists there have got so good at reading

the signals that they can distinguish between the jubilation of home-team wins and the muted celebrations of away-team goals.

They can also tell when the stadium is being used for concerts – and work out whether people are rocking to death metal or bopping to a pop band.

They are sensing waves. And what waves are – whether sound waves, light waves, radio waves, or, in this case, seismic waves – is energy on the move. Sometimes, a lot of energy.

THE LISBON EARTHQUAKE

In 1755, a terrible earthquake struck Lisbon, in Portugal. Tens of thousands died as the city was shaken to rubble.

The shaking that caused this was moving energy. In the Earth's crust, there had been a judder, a sudden release of energy as plates of rock ground against each other.

Energy has to go somewhere – it can't just stay stuck in one place. So that energy had travelled as waves, the same type of waves created by Barcelona's goals. And as these waves passed through the ground, they shook it.

Some of those waves, in Barcelona and in Lisbon, were **transverse** waves, vibrating side-to-side. These look like waves in the sea.

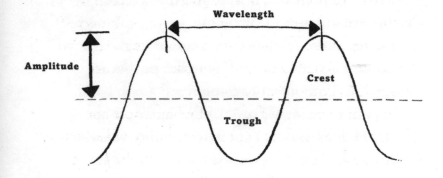

Others were **longitudinal** waves, vibrating along their direction of travel.

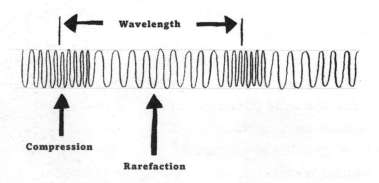

They were not the only waves created though – there are many ways for energy to spread.

As the ground shook in Lisbon, it vibrated the air, creating sound waves, which meant that people heard the crack and judder of buildings collapsing and the Earth moving.

Out at sea it created a water wave – a tsunami – that spread through the Atlantic Ocean. A thousand kilometres away, on the south coast of England, this wave reached land, tearing down the homes of petrified residents of Cornwall.

Most of them would never learn the cause, or guess that a little bit of the terrible energy unleashed on Lisbon had transported itself through the sea, a messenger of destruction from Portugal.

POSITIVE WAVES

Waves can be killers, but without them we would be nothing.

While the point of waves, as far as Physics is concerned, is to transfer energy, their purpose for humans can be very different. Because we have hijacked waves for our own ends.

When we talk we create a little controlled burst of energy in our voice box in the form of vibrations, and waves in the air carry it to our listeners.

The different sounds have different **frequencies** (which is a word for the number of waves passing a point in a given time), and we use this to convey information.

What we see with our eyes is energy from the sun, better known as light waves, bouncing off materials or being absorbed by them.

With specific sorts of waves – those at certain frequencies – humans are very good at spotting the slight changes and then giving them names.

So, for instance, if the air vibrates 261.6 times a second, we say it is the sound of middle C.

If an object reflects only light in which the tops of waves are a tenth of the width of a human hair apart, we call it "yellow".

If, say, there is a regular patterned fluctuation in that "yellow", we might decide the object doing the reflecting is fur.

And if it has four legs and bounds towards us, we can call the yellow furry thing a Labrador and let it lick us.

UNWEAVING THE RAINBOW

John Keats was an English poet who liked to spend his time mooning after unobtainable women, writing over-long verse about the mellow fruitfulness of autumn and moping his way around the countryside being sickly.*

But one day, somewhat unexpectedly, he decided to branch out by insulting the greatest scientist his country had ever produced.

Isaac Newton, he declared, was soulless. In describing how light could be split into its constituent parts, Newton had "unweaved the rainbow".

*Or, at least, that not wholly-objective view is how it seems to someone who had to study him at great length for A-level.

In showing that the ethereal beauty of a rainbow was precisely described by the differential bending of light, he had removed the mystery of a natural phenomenon and replaced it with the cold, calculations of Physics.

It would be nice to think that had Newton been alive, he would have quietly sat down Keats, and shown him how wrong he was. He would have demonstrated that the beauty of a rainbow is only heightened by the intellectual delight of knowing how it works.

It would be nice to say that, but it's obviously nonsense. As you now know, Newton was a weirdo who disliked most people and was so against the idea of explaining his work that he deliberately made it too obscure even for many mathematicians to understand.

And, obviously, Keats – a man who once declared "truth is beauty, beauty truth, that is all you need to know" – was unlikely to have been patient with the idea that, as well as beauty, he also needed to know about angles.

But let's imagine they did have that conversation. How do you unweave a rainbow? It turns out that to do so requires learning some of the most crucial concepts in waves.

Light travels slower in water than in light. This means that if it hits at an angle it is "refracted": it changes direction.

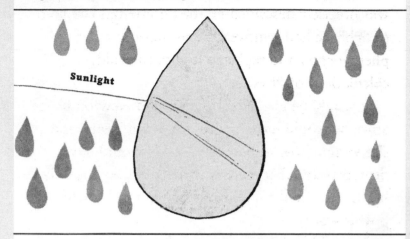

But a ray of white light is actually made up of rays of light of lots of different wavelengths — from red to violet. These different wavelengths are refracted to different degrees — meaning that on entering the water the red light bends less than violet light. So the white light ray spreads out, and appears as different colours.

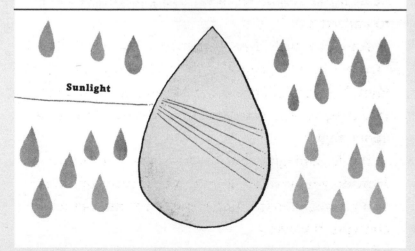

Light does not only refract, it reflects. This means that, just as in a mirror, it bounces off a surface. This is what happens to some of the light when it hits the barrier between the raindrop and the air. Instead of going through it comes back.

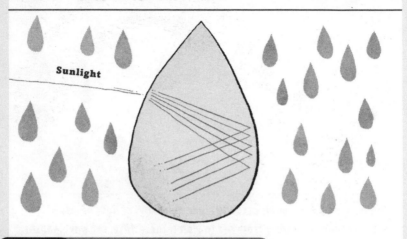

Just as when it came into the raindrop, on the way out it refracts again — spreading out the light into its different colours even more

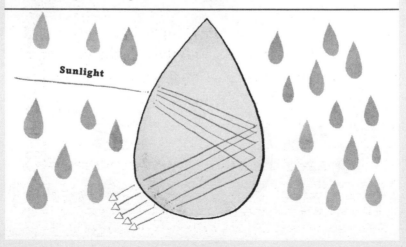

142

So every raindrop is sending out these mini rainbows. Why, then, do you see a semicircle in the sky? Why isn't the whole sky a big psychedelic rainbow — as each raindrop refracts and splits the Sun's light?

The answer is, it is — but most of that light misses you. Only a thin band of raindrops send you a rainbow — and each of those only send you one colour.

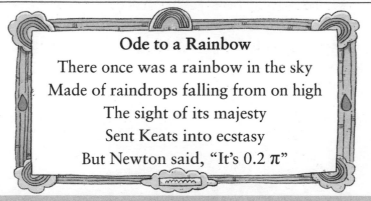

Ode to a Rainbow
There once was a rainbow in the sky
Made of raindrops falling from on high
The sight of its majesty
Sent Keats into ecstasy
But Newton said, "It's 0.2 π"

0.2 π is another way of saying 42 degrees (or thereabouts — it's actually 0.23 π, but that doesn't scan as well in the limerick), in a system called RADIANS. Sometimes mathematicians find it useful to consider that a full circle is not 360 degrees, but 2 π radians.

143

LENSES

In 1691 Robert Boyle, the scientist, sat down and made some predictions for humanity's future.

Among these were that humans would be able to "Attain Gigantick Dimensions", design "A Ship to saile with All Winds, and A Ship not to be Sunk" (1 out of 2 isn't bad), and – showing how excited Britain was by the arrival of a new-fangled drink from India – "Freedom from Necessity of much Sleeping exemplify'd by the Operations of Tea".

A fourth prediction was almost as fantastical: "The making of Parabolicall and Hyperbolicall Glasses."

He thought that in the future, everyone who needed it would benefit from one of the most astonishing inventions of the Middle Ages – glasses.

Glasses work because of lenses, which can subtly change the path of light to compensate for faults in your eye.

And lenses work because of refraction – the same thing that goes on in a raindrop.

CONCAVE LENSES

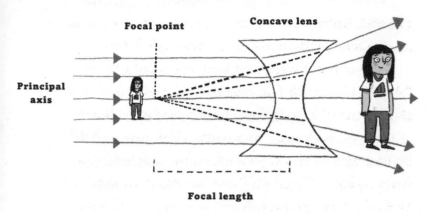

A concave lens takes light and spreads it, making things seem bigger.

CONVEX LENSES

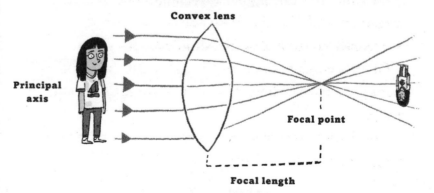

A convex lens can do the reverse, focusing light to make them smaller. After it has focused light to a point, the rays cross, the image goes upside down, and eventually it gets bigger again.

Light does not stop at the edges of a rainbow. The colours we see are just a tiny band of what is known as the **electromagnetic spectrum**.

Some animals can see other parts. Bees buzz around in a world where ultraviolet light – with a shorter wavelength than anything we can see – is visible. Snakes slither in a world with infrared light that has a longer wavelength and is made by hot things. (That is how they spot warm-blooded mice.)

Some parts are invisible to everything, but that does not mean they are useless. Instead, they can be used to heat your food, as microwaves, or enable you to listen to music while you wait for your lunch to cook, as the even-longer-wavelength radio waves.

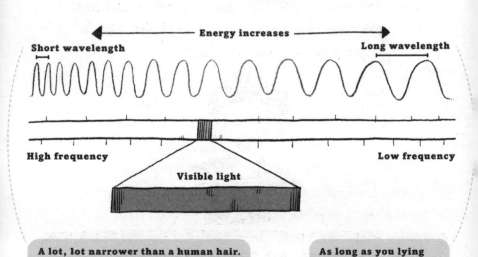

Energy increases

Short wavelength   Long wavelength

High frequency   Low frequency

Visible light

A lot, lot narrower than a human hair. These waves are used in things like hospital X-rays, to see your bones.

As long as you lying down. These waves are used in radios and TVs.

The amount of light a substance absorbs and emits varies from object to object. Emitting light is different to reflecting it – which is what happens when it simply bounces back straight away. Light that is absorbed is converted to heat energy, and light that is emitted is normally bounced back as infrared light. Something that absorbs all frequencies on the electromagnetic spectrum is called a **"black body"**.

The name is not metaphorical. There is a reason why a black t-shirt on a hot day feels hot: it absorbs a lot of light energy. The temperature of an object is governed by the difference between how much light it absorbs and how much it emits.

The hotter it gets, the more infrared light (which you can't see) it produces. And if it gets really hot, the light it emits may even be visible light. That's why we have the phrase "red hot".

IN SHORT: Waves are how you wave goodbye to energy.

WHAT YOU NEED TO KNOW:

- Waves are moving energy. They can be **transverse** (side to side) or **longitudinal** (back and forth).
- They can reflect, when they bounce off things, or refract – which means their path gets displaced as they move into a different medium.
- Light is an **electromagnetic wave**, part of a spectrum ranging from the long wavelength radio waves to short wavelength gamma rays.
- Using the rules of refraction, light can be manipulated with lenses.
- The temperature of an object can be linked to the difference between the electromagnetic radiation emitted and absorbed.

WHAT YOU DON'T NEED TO KNOW, BUT MIGHT LIKE TO:
WAVE-PARTICLE DUALITY

Imagine you are standing at the beach, watching the waves come in.

I can do that. This already sounds much more promising than our usual conversations.

You see the wave rise, foam, and begin to break.

Again, this is sensible. Waves are reasonable. Waves I understand.

Then just as it is about to crash onto the beach, all of the wave disappears except at one point – where a great blob of energy suddenly materializes and digs a big hole in the sand.

Sigh.

That's like light.

No it's not.

Unfortunately, it really is.

Go on then. You might as well ruin both light and the seaside for me at the same time.

For 1,000 years, physicists had been debating light. Is it a particle, or is it a wave?

Wave, clearly wave. You've spent nearly a whole chapter describing how it's a wave.

And it is one. That's obvious. It will refract, reflect, and interfere with itself just like a wave. It has a wavelength, it waves around like a wave.

It is, all in all, extremely wavy.

Great, let's stop.

But sometimes it's also a particle.

If you fire light at a solar panel, for instance, it converts it into electricity in a way only possible if light is a particle. It is like it arrives in separate, countable, packets of energy.

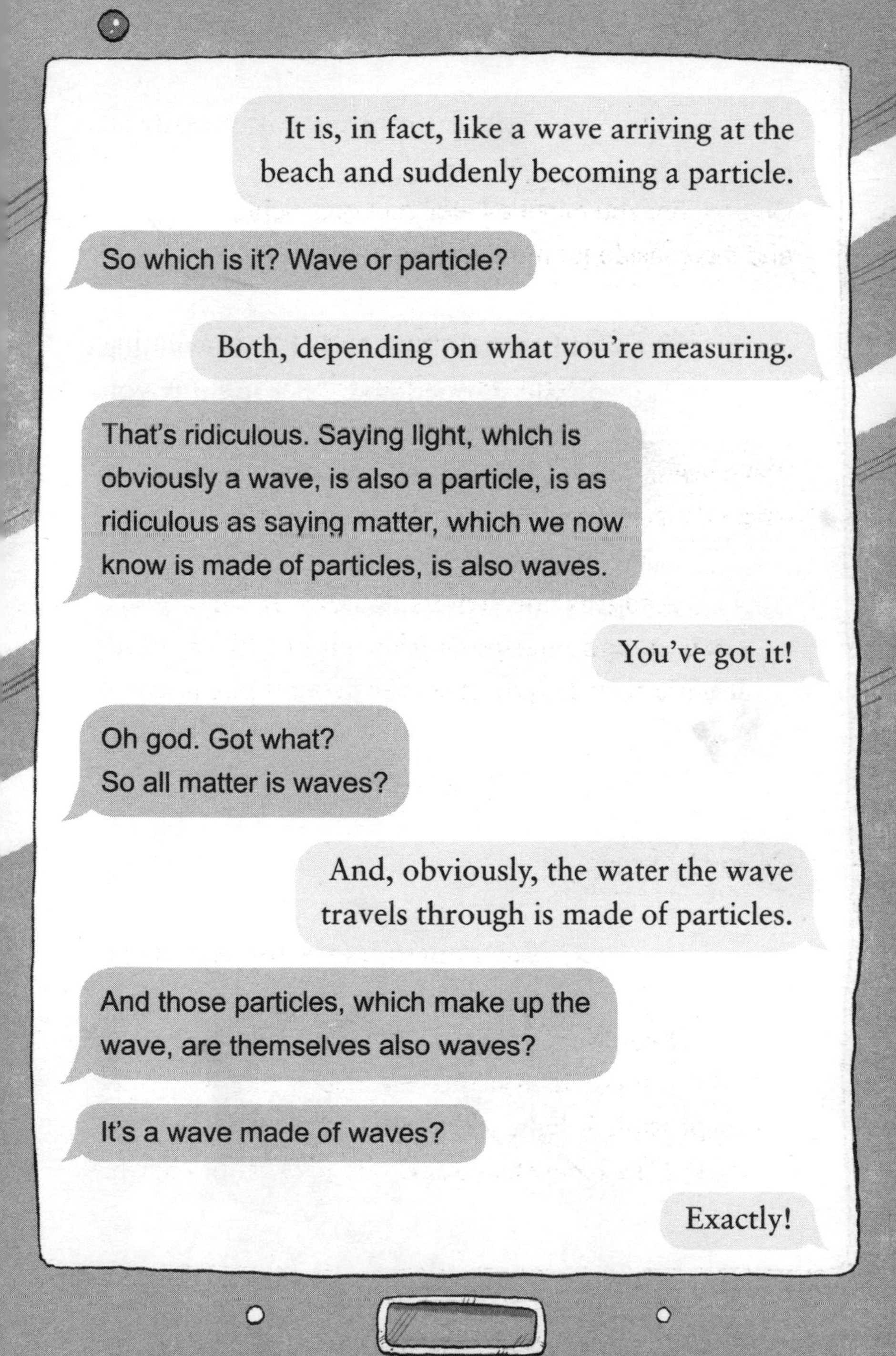
It is, in fact, like a wave arriving at the beach and suddenly becoming a particle.
So which is it? Wave or particle?
Both, depending on what you're measuring.
That's ridiculous. Saying light, which is obviously a wave, is also a particle, is as ridiculous as saying matter, which we now know is made of particles, is also waves.
You've got it!
Oh god. Got what?
So all matter is waves?
And, obviously, the water the wave travels through is made of particles.
And those particles, which make up the wave, are themselves also waves?
It's a wave made of waves?
Exactly!

None of that makes any sense.

Good, admitting that is the first step.

Richard Feynman, the Nobel Prize-winning physicist, once said, "If you think you understand quantum mechanics, you don't understand quantum mechanics."

Phew. Does that mean if I say that I don't understand quantum mechanics, I'm as clever as Feynman?

No.

CHAPTER 7

ELECTRO-MAGNETISM

INTRODUCTION
ELECTROMAGNETISM

IN THIS CHAPTER YOU WILL LEARN ABOUT:

- Magnets
- Magnetic fields
- Electromagnets
- Motors and generators

When the Roman naturalist Pliny the Elder first saw a magnet, he said, "What phenomenon is more astonishing? Where has nature shown greater audacity?"

Unlike Pliny, for whom much of the world was a mystery, we have a lot more knowledge we can use to understand magnets, and how they are made.

Some comes from Chapter Four. When electricity flows it creates magnetism – something we can use to create powerful electromagnets, and even more powerful motors.

Some comes from Chapter Five. The reason that magnets are so useful at all is because of the force they exert.

Today, magnets are something we stick on the fridge. The idea that they are near-mystical objects seems preposterous.

But maybe it shouldn't be. A lot of very clever people have been fascinated and perplexed by magnets – and still are.

THE WONDER OF MAGNETS

A thousand years ago, Chinese military tacticians were thrilled by an astonishing new navigation device: a metal object shaped like a fish.

No longer did generals need to fear night-time manoeuvres, nor worry about getting lost on cloudy days. Instead, they could just rely on the services of what they called their "south-pointing fish".

The instructions for using the fish were simple – just place it, floating, in a bowl of water and it slowly spun around to face south (or north, depending on which end you considered the "front").

The fish must have seemed like magic. It was actually almost as fantastical – a link to the centre of the Earth, through magnetism.

Six thousand kilometres below the feet of the Chinese generals was the magnetized core of the Earth.

The fish, a magnet too, could seek this fellow magnet out and align with it. It could tune into the field lines that spread from its top, in the direction of the North Pole, and its bottom, in the direction of the South Pole.

It was the world's first compass.

HOW DID IT WORK?

If you aren't amazed by magnets, you haven't been thinking about them hard enough. One person who did think about them was Albert Einstein.

All his adult life, he said he remembered seeing a compass aged four – that compass, he later wrote, was his first inkling that there was "something behind things, something deeply hidden".

While the Chinese generals used their magnetic fish to see deep into the Earth, in that magnetized needle, Einstein saw deep into the universe.

SURELY MAGNETS AREN'T THAT COMPLEX?

Here is the explanation you may have heard for magnets. Inside a magnetic material – the most common one we think about is iron – there are "domains".

These are like little magnets. Each one has a north and south pole, like the Earth's poles.

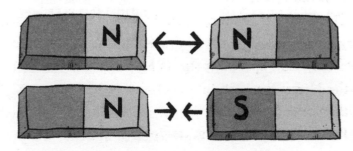

Like poles repel each other, opposite poles attract.

This means that a normal magnet will create a magnetic field that repels the same poles, attracts opposite ones and also attracts other magnetic materials.

All the different domains make a magnetic material, a little like a box of jumbled-up magnets. The box is not itself a magnet – so as long as all the magnets inside are pointing in different directions they cancel each other out.

But if you rub another magnet over the box, and it's powerful enough, you can make all the little magnets align.

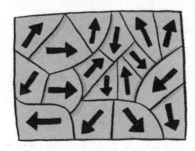 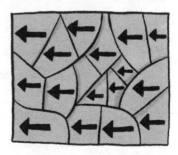

Domains are jumbled, cancelling out each other.   **Domains align, and the material becomes magnetic.**

They effectively join together into one big magnet.

"Hard" magnets are those then stay magnetized afterwards.

"Soft" magnets are those that lose their magnetism when they are not in the presence of another magnet.

SO THAT'S HOW MAGNETS WORK THEN?

Sort of. Except you don't have to be a professor of logic to see the teensiest flaw in that explanation – the reason why so many scientists still find magnets so fascinating.

If you say that a magnet is something made out of smaller magnets, you haven't really explained a magnet at all.

The key is explaining the smaller magnets – the domains. And that is a lot harder.

The reason domains exist is because inside them are lots of atoms, and inside each atom there are electrons whizzing around.

Those electrons are themselves like little magnets and, in a domain, all the electrons on average align – meaning those whizzing magnets can together create a magnetic field.

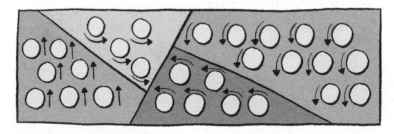

Domains each have electrons acting in unison.

All of which just leaves two small questions:

1. Why do the electrons line up in domains in magnetic materials, and ...
2. Why are the electrons like little magnets?

And that's when you realize that even this explanation is an even more complicated way of saying "a magnet is a magnet because it is made of smaller magnets".

ELECTROMAGNETISM

This explanation of magnets is, at best, only half way to telling us why the Chinese fish pointed south. We know the fish was magnetic, but why was the Earth?

To consider this you have to understand a different kind of magnetism entirely: **electromagnetism**.

Around the iron core beneath the Chinese generals' feet, there were – and still are – swirling eddies of molten metal. As the Earth turns, this constant motion is maintained.

This creates an electric current, as electrons swirl around the superheated soup. Electricity and

magnetism, scientists now realize, are in some ways two sides of the same phenomenon.

Magnets can be explained by understanding that electrons sometimes act in synchrony.

Nowhere are electrons more synchronous than in electricity – so it should not be surprising that all electric currents create a magnetic force as they flow.

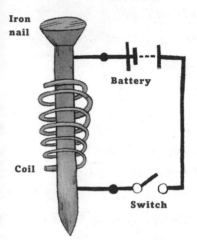

Iron nail

Battery

Coil

Switch

If they flow around a big lump of iron – whether at 6,000 degrees Celsius in the Earth's core or a nail – they create something else: an electromagnet.

Electromagnets have two great virtues that mean you can now find them everywhere – from loud speakers to medical scanners.

The first is that they can be far more powerful than normal magnets.

The second is that they are magnets you can switch on and off.

Provided, obviously, that the electromagnet in question isn't a white-hot lump of metal beneath a turbulent ocean of lava.

ANIMAL MAGNETISM

You don't have to have a
compass to navigate. All
you need is a dog that
needs the toilet.

Scientists know that
some animals, such as
homing pigeons, can sense
magnetism – that is almost
certainly how many of
them are able to navigate
long distances.

But one of the most unusual demonstrations of
this came in 2014, when one group of researchers
claimed that dogs can too. And they came to this
conclusion by watching them poo.

Across 2,000 separate pooing incidents, they
found that a defecating dog was more likely to
align its bottom in a north-south direction.

They suggest that dogs retain some of the
skills they once had as wolves, when they had to
travel over a huge area to hunt. In some way, they
suspected, the dogs "see" the Earth's magnetic
field.

Then when they feel the urge, they multitask –
and check their bearings as well.

WHEN NORTH ISN'T NORTH

In 2014, North moved. For the first time in 350 years, the Ordnance Survey (Britain's official mapping company) amended all of its maps to recognize that compasses no longer point where they should.

"Magnetic north" has always been slightly different to "true north" – which is the point on the Earth farthest from the equator. But now it is on the move.

Deep underground, in the swirling currents of magma that surround the Earth's core, something is shifting. The magnetic poles of the planet are changing – and no one is entirely sure why.

It might be a small correction. But it might be something worse. The fear is that the Earth's magnet might be preparing to flip entirely.

We know this happens every few hundred thousand years, we know it last happened a few hundred thousand years ago, and we know that if it does flip it will be an event that won't just confuse migrating birds and defecating dogs, but every human device that depends on a compass too.

THE MOTOR EFFECT

La Jamais Contente is French for The Never Satisfied. It is also the name of a car owned by a man who was himself never satisfied – and who entered the record books because of it.

Camille Jenatzy was known as the Red Devil because of the way his red beard blurred into a demonic whizz as his car sped past.

Three times he became the fastest human in a car, and on the third occasion he broke another record too – in *La Jamais Contente*, he was the first person to drive faster than 100 kilometres an hour.

Back then the car's success was attributed to its streamlined shape – it was basically a torpedo on wheels. Few commented on the power source it used to achieve these astonishing speeds: electricity.

After all, in 1900 all the fastest cars used electricity. And why wouldn't they?

When you have something as gloriously simple as an electric motor, why would you do something as absurd as rely on an internal combustion engine – a machine that literally harnesses explosions to move you forward?

An electric motor is one of the most elegant machines devised by humans. It works because of the one simple fact that makes electromagnets work too – electricity creates a magnetic field.

1 The current flowing round the coil makes a magnetic field that is misaligned with the one made by the magnets. It wants to turn 180 degrees, so the two are not opposed.

2 As it turns, the bit touching the commutator also turns. The wires from the battery brush against it, passing current.

3 When it turns too far, the half of the commutator that was originally touching the positive side of the circuit moves to the negative. Suddenly the current in the magnetic field reverses.

4 Once again, the coil makes a magnetic field that opposes the one in the magnets – and so it keeps on turning.

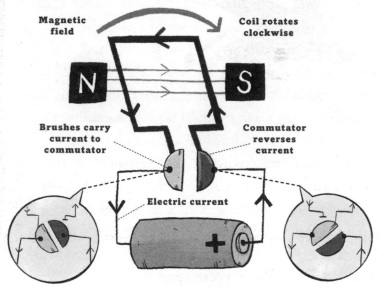

Magnetic field

Coil rotates clockwise

N   S

Brushes carry current to commutator

Commutator reverses current

Electric current

The amazing thing about learning about motors is that, through this, you can also understand generators. A motor takes electrical energy and turns it into rotation; a generator is just that, in reverse. It takes rotation and, by turning a coil in a magnetic field, makes electricity. This electricity is **electromagnetically induced.**

FLEMING'S LEFT-HAND RULE

To work out which direction the wire gets pushed in a motor, use Fleming's left-hand rule.*

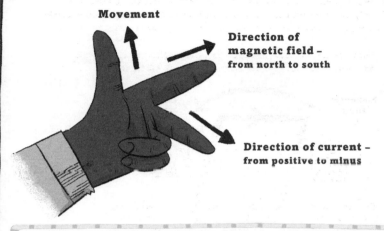

Movement

Direction of magnetic field –
from north to south

Direction of current –
from positive to minus

*It actually works with any left hand. Which is lucky because the left hand of Fleming, who died in 1945, is pretty decomposed these days.

THE WRONG ENGINE WON

If the electric motor is so beautiful and superior, why do we mostly drive engines powered by petrol – a fuel that, apart from anything else, is bad for our lungs and the environment?

The answer is not the engine, but the fuel. A kilogram of petrol carried well over a hundred times the energy of a kilogram of the batteries used then.

Even today, with significantly more efficient batteries, petrol has around forty times more energy stored in it.

Eventually Jenatzy, who became famous through electric cars, switched to racing in petrol ones. But he never completely trusted them – he apparently predicted he would die in a Mercedes Benz.

It was not, in the end, the racing that got him. One day in 1913 he was out hunting and decided to play a practical joke on his friends. He hid in a bush and made animal sounds.

His joke was too effective – they thought he really was an animal and shot him. Realizing their mistake, they rushed him to hospital. Unfortunately, he died in the car on the way.

That car? A Mercedes Benz.

IN SHORT: Magnets are our link to the centre of the Earth, the secrets of the universe and the structure of the atom.

And they aren't too shabby at sticking things on your fridge.

WHAT YOU NEED TO KNOW:

- A magnet has a **north** and **south pole** that are created by the direction of its magnetic field. Like poles **repel**, opposite poles **attract** – meaning that the north end of one magnet will be attracted to the south end of another.
- Magnets create a **magnetic field**, which attracts other magnetic materials such as iron.
- This is not the only form of magnetism. Electric current creates its own magnetic field.
- If you coil a wire around a magnetic material, you create an **electromagnet** that you can switch on and off by passing a current through it.
- A wire carrying electricity in a magnetic field will feel a force trying to move it. Exploiting this is the way that motors work – and the way electricity is generated.

> One day, in a laboratory in Nottingham, some scientists put a couple of really big magnets beneath a frog – and it levitated.

That must have been pretty surprising?

> On the one hand, nothing in the frog's previous experience would have prepared it for floating around above a magnet. But, on the other hand, it was a frog – so who knows?

No – surprising for the scientists, I mean!

Not at all, it was just what they expected to happen.

But weren't they at least a little shocked to find out that frogs are magnetic?

> They're not.

Then why did this one levitate?
Had it swallowed a nail?

Because frogs are diamagnetic.

Diamag-what-ic?

Diamagnetic. Magnetism is actually extremely odd – diamagnetism is far more common. Diamagnetism is the name for a kind of electromagnetism.

How does it work?

Think of an atom. Orbiting around the nucleus are electrons. Orbiting electrons are moving. And moving electrons are…?

Electricity?

Exactly. So it's a mini electric current. Now imagine you put a magnet near by.

That would mean there is a current moving in …

… a magnetic field.

And that makes a force?

Exactly! One that repels the magnet – and lifts frogs.

And what objects are diamagnetic, other than frogs?

Any with moving electrons in. All of them in other words. The only reason we don't notice this is the effect is very, very small – so you only see it with extremely powerful magnets.

Hang on, so anything – a carrot, say, or an apple – would be similarly diamagnetic?

Yes.

Then why did they feel the need to bother a frog?

Because it's funnier.

CHAPTER 8

COSMOLOGY

INTRODUCTION
COSMOLOGY

IN THIS CHAPTER YOU WILL LEARN ABOUT:

- The solar system
- The life cycle of a star
- Red shift
- Orbit
- The Big Bang
- ... and the fate of the universe!

BEFORE YOU READ THIS CHAPTER:

"Who are we?" asked the American astronomer Carl Sagan. "We find that we live on an insignificant planet of a humdrum star, lost in a galaxy, tucked away in some forgotten corner of a universe, in which there are far more galaxies than people."

Space is immense. It is huger, and quite possibly stranger, than humans are built to imagine. It is easy to feel not just insignificant, but utterly adrift...

Which is, perhaps, why this – the final chapter – relies on so much you have already learnt. Here, as we learn about stars, planets, red shift, orbits and the fate of everything that has ever or will ever exist, you may need to refer back to earlier chapters.

Because to understand it means understanding about the particle theory of matter, energy, waves and a little bit of radiation.

It can feel overwhelming, when faced with the immensity and complexity of the universe.

There is another, more positive way to think of space though. As another astronomer, Jocelyn Bell Burnell, put it, we are not separate from the universe at all. Most of the atoms in us started in stars.

"There is stardust in your veins," she said. "We are literally, ultimately, children of the stars."

THE SOLAR SYSTEM

The universe is the word for everything we know that exists.

Most of the universe is empty, but inside it, just occasionally, you find clumps of more interesting stuff, called galaxies. There are a few hundred billion of these. We are in a galaxy called the Milky Way.

Most of a galaxy is also empty, but fly around it and you will sometimes bump into massive fiery objects called stars. There are a few hundred billion of these in most galaxies.

Our star is called the Sun. And the Earth, which orbits around it, is part of its solar system – the planets stuck in its gravitational pull.

Every diagram you have ever seen of the Solar System is almost certainly wrong. They are wrong because space is too big for books. Space is too big for posters. Space is too big even for massive banners that stretch the length of a classroom.

Space contains far, far too much space. More than that, the bits that aren't space – planets and stars – are far, far too big.

So we cheat. We crunch and we shuffle and we squeeze things up so that space (which is big) can be understood by our brains (which are small).

Here, in no particular order, are the things that are wrong with diagrams of the Solar System:

1. **The planets are all in a big line.**
   Planets do not end up in big lines. Not only is it highly implausible, it would cause the world's astrologers – who build careers on making barmy assertions in newspaper horoscopes – to go supernova with excitement.

   In reality, planets are spread about across the face of a big circle, orbiting like they are following the grooves in an old vinyl record.

2. **Jupiter is too small.**
   The actual Jupiter is so big that you could fit 1,300 Earths inside it.

   It is heavier than all the other planets combined, twice over. It is so big it has a storm that is wider than the Earth and has raged for centuries.

   This is a very, very big planet.

3. Everything is far too scrunched up.
   It looks like the distance from Earth to Mars is one Jupiter-width.

   Even allowing for the fact that this Jupiter is far too small, Earth and Mars are actually 500 Jupiters apart.

4. The Solar System actually stretches all the way to the Oort cloud, an icy band of comets far, far beyond Pluto.

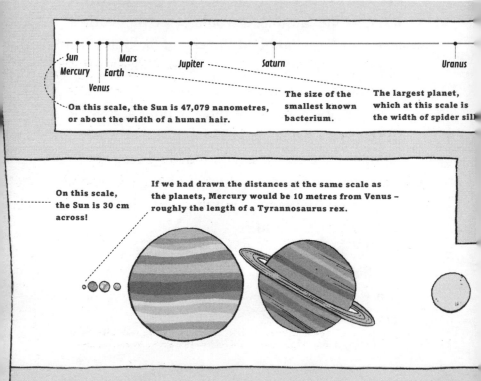

Sun
Mercury
Venus
Mars
Earth
Jupiter
Saturn
Uranus

On this scale, the Sun is 47,079 nanometres, or about the width of a human hair.

The size of the smallest known bacterium.

The largest planet, which at this scale is the width of spider silk

On this scale, the Sun is 30 cm across!

If we had drawn the distances at the same scale as the planets, Mercury would be 10 metres from Venus – roughly the length of a Tyrannosaurus rex.

In fact, if you are reading this in your living room and Pluto is the edge of the page, the Oort cloud would be comfortably outside your front door – and probably halfway along the road.

The edge of the Oort cloud is about 2,000 times further out than Pluto.

So here is an actual scale diagram of the Solar System, drawn so that everything will fit on the page. Exciting, isn't it?

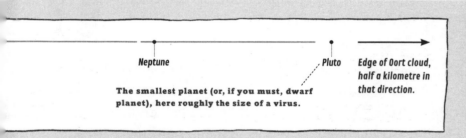

Neptune   · Pluto   Edge of Oort cloud,
half a kilometre in
that direction.

The smallest planet (or, if you must, dwarf
planet), here roughly the size of a virus.

What, that's not that useful? Here's another diagram, with the planets drawn at scale and big enough to be visible – and the distances between using a different scale.

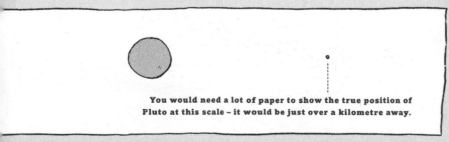

You would need a lot of paper to show the true position of
Pluto at this scale – it would be just over a kilometre away.

A COSMIC DEMOTION

One day, after 4 billion years minding its own business orbiting the Sun, Pluto was no longer a planet.

It hadn't changed, we had – an arbitrary decision by the International Astronomical Union deemed it too small, and a "dwarf planet".

PIONEER 10

The first human-made interstellar object was Pioneer 10. It was launched in 1972, and after visiting Jupiter and the asteroid belt it continued into deep space.

NASA put a gold plaque on it giving basic details about Earth and humans in case, after travelling for millions of years to the next star system, it was ever found by an alien civilization.

At the time, there was a minor controversy because the humans on the plaque were naked – which offended some humans, if not (one presumes) aliens.

URANUS

In 1781 the astronomer William Herschel spotted a new planet. He wanted to call it "George", after his king. That was considered a silly name for a planet though, so a considerably more sensible and in no way unintentionally amusing name was chosen: Uranus.

ORBIT

Experienced trackers
can use the subtle signs
of the forest to navigate.
The position of moss on
trees, or the positions of
spiderwebs, can tell them
which way is north.

For the urban tracker,
lost on their way to
the bus stop, there are
equally subtle signs –
and the clearest are
satellite dishes.

Satellite dishes always point to the equator.
That means if you are in the Northern Hemisphere,
where Britain is, they point south. In the Southern
Hemisphere they point north. On the equator itself
they point up. (Which is less useful – if you don't
know which way up is, you really are lost.)

The reason they point to the equator is
because, in space, that's where the TV satellites
are. That's where they can be something called
"geostationary".

To understand what that is though, you have
to understand orbit.

FALLING BUT NEVER LANDING

Orbit is not really weightlessness. There is still gravity in space.

The reason astronauts float around is not because gravity has gone, it's because they are falling. They are falling all the time, but never hitting the ground.

This sounds strange, but it is quite easy to understand – you just have to remember that the Earth is round.

Imagine you threw a ball from a mountain, really hard and fast – and imagine there was no air to slow it down.

The ball would go a long way, but gravity would eventually make it fall towards the Earth until it hit the ground.

Imagine you threw it a bit harder so that it moved a bit faster. It would go further, and curve round over the horizon a bit further as it fell.

Finally, imagine you threw it so hard that it followed the same curve as the Earth. It would come all the way round and hit you on the head.

That's orbit (without, normally, the head-wound).

Now think about television satellites. Just like that ball they orbit around the Earth, zooming over our heads.

Except, think how annoying it would be if your satellite dish had to follow them as they orbited – tracking them across the sky.

So they don't. TV satellites do something really clever – they are put at a height where their orbit takes 24 hours: one day.

There is something else that takes 24 hours to spin … the Earth itself. As well as going around the Sun in orbit, it turns on its own axis, and each day is one spin.

This means that TV satellites orbit the Earth above the equator at exactly the speed the Earth spins, so your satellite dishes always point to the same place. They are moving, but so are we.

In fact everything, ultimately, is in orbit. Satellites orbit us, we orbit the Sun, and the Sun and all the other stars in the Milky Way orbit its centre – and will do until the end of the universe.

Or, depending on their size, until they explode...

LIFE CYCLE OF A STAR

Stars are the reason the universe has meaning.

Stars, we all know, provide the heat and light that allow life to be sustained. While they are doing that they also do something just as important, but which amid the dazzle of their light often goes unnoticed.

They create the elements that mean life can exist at all.

The carbon in the paper of this book, the iron in the blood pumping round your body, the nitrogen in the DNA in each of your cells, the calcium in the bones of the fingers that turn the page – all of it comes from a star that died billions of years ago.

Probably, in fact, from several stars. You exist because stars die. But before they die, they have to be born.

Stars start life as a loose collection of trillions of particles, brought together by their gravity.

As they come together the particles spin, orbiting around a central core, drawing closer and closer and becoming hotter and hotter. Eventually, they become so hot that fusion can occur.

This is the point when hydrogen atoms – the simplest, lightest, and most common atoms there are – join together to make helium atoms.

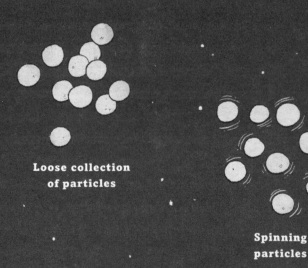

Loose collection
of particles

Spinning
particles

Crucially, one helium atom is just ever so slightly less heavy than the hydrogen atoms that make it. 0.71 per cent of their mass is lost, and converted to a huge amount of energy in the process.

For some smaller stars, such as our own, this process will be their destiny.

They will slowly convert their hydrogen into helium; then, when it runs out, they will give a great stellar shrug – expanding to be a red giant before gracefully accepting their eventual fate as a dim, small, white dwarf.

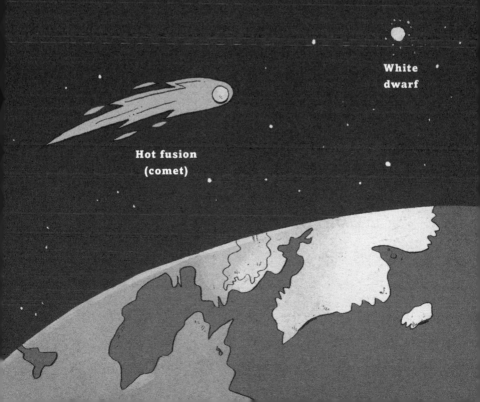

White dwarf

Hot fusion
(comet)

THE LIFE OF A STAR

PROTOSTAR

MAIN SEQUENCE STAR

STARS ABOUT AS LARGE AS THE SUN

STARS MUCH LARGER THAN THE SUN

RED GIANT STAR

RED SUPER GIANT STAR

WHITE DWARF

SUPERNOVA

BLACK DWARF

BLACK HOLE

NEUTRON STAR

A DIGRESSION: A GLOSSARY OF STARS

- **Main sequence star:** Stars like our own. Minding their own business converting hydrogen to helium.
- **Red giant:** Big and red, as the name suggests. They have run out of hydrogen to fuse into helium in their core, and are now only undergoing fusion with what little fuel remains up towards their surface.
- **White dwarf:** Small and white – physicists like to be literal. With no fuel left, this is a star that is very slowly cooling. It is the core of a red giant.
- **Neutron star:** The collapsed remnants of a very, very big star – squeezed into a ball less than the width of London across. It is so dense that a teaspoon's worth of its matter would weigh 10 million tonnes.
- **Black hole:** Like a neutron star but denser – so dense that even light cannot escape. Black holes are where Physics as we know it ceases, a bottomless hole in space and time that sucks in matter to squish it to a single point of infinite density. So don't fall into one.

THE DEATH OF STARS

The gradual cooling of a white dwarf might sound like a peaceful way to go, but for anyone on the Earth at the time, this process will feel rather less gentle.

Nearby planets will disappear into its growing bulk with the brief protesting sizzle of an ant caught in a lava flow. But it will be nothing compared to the violence of a larger star's death.

When bigger stars run out of hydrogen, they become supernovae. In one of the most cataclysmic events in the universe, they burn briefly with the light of 100 million suns.

Inside the star, the nuclear fusion process runs out of control. Just as hydrogen joins to make helium, so in this last phase the helium joins to make heavier elements, which then join to make heavier elements still – before it is too much for the star to contain.

It ejects all these elements in one last blast, a stellar rain of exotic elements in the final dazzling brightness of its death throes. Then, all that is left behind is an extremely dense core that becomes a neutron star or a black hole.

Meanwhile, the ejected particle debris spreads across the galaxy, finding its way into other stars, asteroids, planets and – eventually – into beings clever enough to understand that, without those atoms, they would not be there at all.

Beings better known to us as humans.

RED SHIFT

It is the smallest of changes.

If you look through a powerful enough telescope at the light from distant galaxies, you will see the faintest of reddenings – just the slightest difference in the energy spectrum radiated from their stars.

And the further away the galaxy is, the greater the reddening becomes.

Astronomers were very excited when they spotted this "red shift" and realized what it meant.

Because it implies one important thing. It suggests that the entirety of our universe – every hope, dream, achievement and love affair there ever was – will end in a cold, lifeless eternity of death and pointlessness.

Stars, you see, are not really redder the further they
are from us. They just look like they are – and the
reason for this, and why scientists got so excited, is
that the universe is expanding.

As the light from stars travels on its long journey
across the universe, the space it is travelling through
stretches ... stretching the light along with it.

Imagine you drew a coloured line on a deflated
balloon, then blew it up. The colour would get
fainter as it stretched, and became spread more
thinly.

If you stretch the universe as a beam of light
travels along it, its colour changes too. As the light
is stretched, its "wavelength" – the distance between
two peaks of a light wave – increases.

And bigger wavelengths mean redder-looking light.

A TINY UNIVERSE

There are two conclusions we can draw from this.

The first is that if the universe is getting bigger, it used to be smaller – and 13.8 billion years ago was so small it didn't exist.

It was just an infinitely dense point from which everything expanded in a Big Bang, the point at which nothing became something and the universe began.

The second is that eventually, scientists cheerily believe, the universe will be so big that the remaining stars can no longer heat it – and everything we know will become frozen for eternity.

APOCALYPSE, HOW?

So is humanity doomed to a chilly extinction in an obsolete universe?

Probably, but there's still hope the theory may be wrong. A substance called dark energy remains poorly understood, and if it works differently from how we now think then there might not be permanent expansion after all.

Instead, the universe could be pulled back together in a Big Crunch, with every galaxy, planet and civilization crushed together into a terrible, fiery globule of unimaginable density.

That's the glass half-full option.

Either way, it won't happen for a very, very long time.

So if you bought this book because of impending exams, I am afraid you still need to revise.

IN SHORT: We are all stardust.

WHAT YOU NEED TO KNOW:

- The planets, in order, are Mercury, Venus, Earth, Mars, Jupiter, Saturn, Uranus, Neptune (and finally Pluto, a dwarf planet).
- They are **orbiting** the Sun, which is a bit like saying they are always falling – but in a circle.
- Stars begin in dust and gas, before clumping together and making energy through **fusion**.
- Small stars like ours burn for a long time, then form a **red giant**, then finally a **white dwarf**.
- Bigger stars form a super-red giant, then go supernova before making either a really dense **neutron star** or a really, really dense **black hole**.
- Light from distant stars appears redder than it should, which implies the universe is expanding.
- If it is expanding as it gets older, that means it used to be smaller.
- The universe was so small, 13.8 billion years ago that it fitted into a single tiny point, from which everything came – in a **Big Bang**.

WHAT YOU DON'T NEED TO KNOW, BUT MIGHT LIKE TO:

DARK MATTER

What does dark matter look like?

> You can't see it – it's dark.

OK. So what does it feel like? Is it spiky? Hard? Soft?

> You can't feel it either.

Can you taste it then? Or hear it?

> Nope.

Right, so…

> I know what you're going to say. You can't see it, hear it, taste it or feel it – so how do we know it exists?

Exactly. Unless you can smell it?

> You can't smell it.

WHY PHYSICS MATTERS

If you've read this book from end to end, you've now covered most of the essentials for your Physics exam – but you've also glimpsed the science that falls outside of your school syllabus.

As you study for your GCSEs, you might wonder why any of this really matters ... how tables and equations relate to normal life. After all, Physics often seems like a huge, abstract subject; a subject which has little to do with our day-to-day existence.

And the people who care about Physics can certainly seem eccentric. There's no better example than the Ancient Greek scientist Archimedes – who, so the story goes, had a great revelation in his bath tub.

Slumping down into the tub, he noticed that the water had risen up. It had been displaced ... and the volume it was displaced by was *exactly* the same as the volume of his body.

Emerging with an excited splash, he realised that water could be used to measure the volume of any irregular solid ... the irregular solid in this case being the body of the world's greatest scientists.

So he ran down the street naked shouting, "Eureka!" (which in Ancient Greek means, "I have it!").

WHY PHYSICS MATTERS
& INDEX

Many men and women would come after Archimedes. Each, standing on one another's shoulders, would see further and deeper into the mysteries of the universe.

They would learn about the smallest things, and the largest things. They would establish rules, laws and proofs that encompassed everything from the tiny electron to the largest black hole.

But they were also people, like you.

So, while you cram for your exams, keep in mind that Physics isn't just a subject of dry equations. It's a subject created by people who wanted to understand not just *how* the world works, but also *why*.

Because, once you understand *why* the world is the way it is, you can begin to change it in extraordinary ways...

Eccentric? Definitely.

But on another day, in 214 BCE, Physics had become a matter of life and death. And Archimedes' brilliant mind was on altogether more serious watery pursuits.

The fleet of the Roman general, Marcellus, was sailing to attack his town, Syracuse. Rather than putting an admiral in charge of its defence, the townspeople had entrusted their fate to a scientist: Archimedes himself.

Artillery at the time was – quite literally – a hit and miss affair. No one understood the mathematics of how objects flew, how the force and angle translated into velocity and range.

Yet sailors reported that the rocks, flung over the city walls, were far more hit than miss. They arced with unerring accuracy, smashing and splintering the ships beyond.

With each volley, great boulders tore through the Roman fleet, sending its soldiers screaming and spluttering to the bottom of the Mediterranean.

Long before, Archimedes had said: "Give me a place to stand and a lever long enough and I will move the world."

Now his levers were in action, and the world was beginning to move.

There are lots of theories though. The two leading ones are that dark matter is made of something called Weakly Interacting Massive Particles, or of Gravitationally Interacting Massive Particles.

Is that…?

Yes, WIMPs or GIMPs.

The existence of dark matter is making a mockery of Physics; the least physicists can do is mock it back.

Well then, how?

Because of gravity. There is not enough normal matter for our galaxies to stay together or behave in the way they do.

They should be spinning apart and flinging planets and stars in all directions.

How would dark matter stop this?

Just by being there.

The best explanation for why galaxies don't break up is that there is a lot of extra matter that we can't see – in fact, four times as much as normal matter.

The gravitational pull of that dark matter would hold everything together.

What is dark matter though?

No one knows. One of the problems of proposing the existence of a particle that can't really be detected ... is it can't really be detected.

INDEX

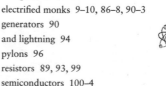

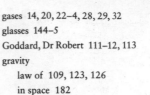

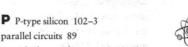
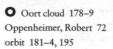

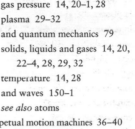
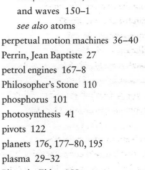

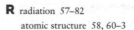

ACKNOWLEDGEMENTS

So many times in writing this book, I have mentally travelled back to my own school days, to the men and women who first tried to explain these concepts to me.

The memory of teachers inevitably stays longer, and sharper, in a child's mind than the child does in the teacher's. Most, probably, will have long forgotten me – but I have not forgotten them, or (some of) the things they taught me.

In making the shift in this book from pupil to teacher, I realized how hard their job is – and how well so many of them did it. So I would like to thank them all, in particular Mr Sharma, Mr Cousins, Mr Perkins and Mr Oakes (teachers, even 25 years on, should not have first names), who guided me through GCSE science, mathematics and beyond. Mr Sharma, who long thought he had marked my last bit of homework, also kindly proofread this. Any mistakes, naturally, are my own.

I would also like to thank Denise Johnstone-Burt and Jane Winterbotham at Walker Books, who came up with the idea, and Jamie Hammond, who was able to make it beautiful in a way that would have entirely eluded me. Talking of beauty, the wonderful illustrations – along with a surprisingly empathetic dinosaur – come from James Davies.

The measure of a good editor is that, when you receive their notes and corrections, you should first believe them to be stupid, then actively malevolent then finally – a few hours later – accept that they were right all along. Becky Watson is a very good editor, and I thank her for her persistence, diligence and unwillingness to let a confusing sentence pass.

Sarah Williams, my agent, continues to corral some fairly eclectic ideas into a form that people might actually want to buy. Her support and advice has been invaluable.

The Times allows me the ridiculous privilege of employing me to chat each day to scientists about their work.

Finally, I would like to thank Catherine. A two-author household that has in the past six years produced twice as many books as children (and hasn't stinted on the children) is not without its stresses. Because of Catherine it has been a collaborative adventure that we have enjoyed together.

TOM WHIPPLE is the science editor at *The Times*. His career has taken him to the top of Mont Blanc and to the tunnels beneath CERN. He has investigated the effects of radiation in the forests around Chernobyl, and the effects of heat in the world's hottest sauna in Finland. He didn't stay in very long. He has reported on three climate change conferences, and only been arrested at one of them. He has a mathematics degree.

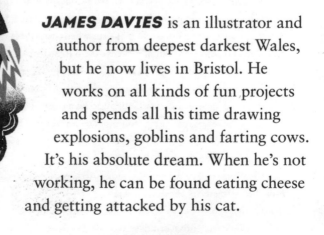

JAMES DAVIES is an illustrator and author from deepest darkest Wales, but he now lives in Bristol. He works on all kinds of fun projects and spends all his time drawing explosions, goblins and farting cows. It's his absolute dream. When he's not working, he can be found eating cheese and getting attacked by his cat.